B.I.B.S.

BIG IDEA BIBLE STUDY

BY RYAN RENCH

Acknowledgements

I heard it my freshman year of Bible college and every year after that: "If you see a turtle on top of a fencepost, you know at least one thing... he didn't get there by himself!"

It is true of all of us. It is true of me. To borrow from Evangelist Billy Ingram—I am a nobody from nowhere with nothing. Anything I *do* have is ultimately from God and is sharpened by others investing in me. While I could acknowledge everyone who has spoken truth into my life, because of the scope of this book, I will limit myself to just a few people.

First, I appreciate Pastor Sam Davison. No one man has shaped my passion for preaching more than my pastor while I was in Bible college. Thank you, Bro. Sam, for your faithfulness in ministry and your passion for God's Word. You have influenced far more people than you will ever care to admit.

Next, in a broad acknowledgment, I thank my classmates at Heartland Baptist Bible College in Oklahoma City, OK. I can think back to particular conversations that shaped my passion and hunger for God's Word, and I learned from my classmates how a disciple of Christ should look and act.

Finally, I thank the Teens of Faith—"my" youth group. They let me claim them as "mine," and they let me practice my preaching on them week after week. This book started as a series of lessons for them. The only reason I think this book has value is because of the depth that developed in them as they were putting these principles into practice. Thank you, Teens of Faith, for granting me a sliver of access into your lives. I take it *very* seriously, and I want to be the absolute best I can be.

CONTENTS

PRELIMINARIES vii
    Foreword By Sam Davison.................................... ix
    From the Author A Word From My Heart.................. xi
    Preface I Wish I'd Had This Tool xv

INTRODUCTION IDEAS IN *GOD'S WORD* 1
    Chapter 1 Knowing God Through His Word 3
    Chapter 2 You Have To Get It 13
    Chapter 3 Why "BIBS?" 19

PART ONE *OBSERVATION* 33
    Chapter 4 OBSERVATION – The Birds-Eye View........ 35
    Chapter 5 Ways To Observe................................ 43

PART TWO *INTERPRETATION* 57
    Chapter 6 INTERPRETATION – What Is God Saying?.... 59
    Chapter 7 First Steps 69
    Chapter 8 The "Trunk" 79
    Chapter 9 The "Branches" 93

PART THREE *APPLICATION* 103
    Chapter 10 APPLICATION – What Is God Saying To Me?...... 105

PART FOUR *CONCLUSION* 113
    Chapter 11 Examples 115
    Chapter 12 Using BIBS.................................... 147
APPENDICES 151
    Appendix 1 Genres – A Deeper Review................... 153
    Appendix 2 Sources.. 187
    Appendix 3 BIBS Devotional Book....................... 189

PRELIMINARIES

FOREWORD

BY SAM DAVISON

Though I had been involved in Bible College work before 1998, the move of Pacific Coast Baptist Bible College to Oklahoma City, OK that year obviously gave me a much different perspective. As I have been involved in Heartland Baptist Bible College, I now have a better position to observe the level of understanding that young men and women from our independent Baptist churches have of the Word of God.

It is that very observation that makes me excited about Ryan Rench's desire and effort to help teens (but not teens alone) actually understand what they read from the Bible and to experience spiritual growth and genuine fellowship with God.

I am in complete agreement with Ryan regarding the plethora of daily devotional guides. It is not as though the serve *no* purpose, I suppose. However, if the use of the daily devotional is pretty much the extent of one's devotional life, then "shallow" would be a word to describe it. Surely God meant for His own—young and old alike—to delight in *His Word*, not in someone's thoughts and stories that may or may not be directly related to His Word.

B.I.B.S. - Big Idea Bible Study

In considering Ryan's work and the BIBS method of devotional Bible study, let me put it this way: If every young person that goes off to Bible College had followed the BIBS method (with some degree of regularity) from fifteen years old to graduation from high school, they would enter the experience a full year ahead (and in some cases, more) of where most enter. Granted, I cannot prove that scientifically. It is my personal observation.

Whether it is the preacher in the pulpit, the Sunday school teacher before a class, the preacher in the retirement home service, ministry in a jail service – whether it's the dorm devotion, family devotion, workplace devotion – whether it's the teen just returned from youth camp, a man just back from a men's retreat, or a lady back from ladies retreat and inspired to read the Bible – whether it's a twelve-year-old or a grandparent sitting to read the Bible – *everyone* will benefit and grow if they will put forth the effort to know what is being said on the pages of the Bible. BIBS can help, big time!

Ryan Rench has given attention to a major theme of our homiletics classes at Heartland Baptist Bible College, which is that we labor to know the intent of the biblical writer, which then gives us the intent of God who inspired the biblical writer. *Everyone* needs to approach the Bible in that way.

I praise God for the number of teens (and others) who will be helped by the Big Idea Bible Study. It will help many to become people of the Bible, indeed!

Bro. Sam Davison
Pastor Emeritus, Southwest Baptist Church, Oklahoma City, OK
President, Heartland Baptist Bible College, Oklahoma City, OK

A Word From My Heart

Teens and the Bible

Ministering to teens is my passion. The Bible is my passion. Combine the two and you have the essence of my current ministry.

As a youth pastor in Southern California, my goal in ministry is no different than a missionary in Europe, a senior pastor in Maine, or a Sunday school teacher in Oklahoma—to help people love God and love others. The people I minister to are different, but the tool we use is the same—God's Word.

I love teens because it was in my teen years that I started to have a relationship with God. I became a Christian when I was five years old, but it was not until late junior high and early high school that I learned what a *personal* relationship with God was.

I want that for every teen I meet.

I want every teen I know to have the sweet fellowship with God that I was able to first get a taste of when I was in high school. I remember being so secure and so full of real joy in high school that it was as if anything could have happened in my life and I would not have had a care in the world.

Not to be morbid, but I remember a conversation I had with a friend that went something like this, "I'm SO serious about this... it's weird, but I'm so good with God right now that it's like I could have peace even if something horrible happened like my mom dying." Now, my mom was not dying (she wasn't even sick), but I was making the point that even *if* some tragedy entered my life, I could trust God with it.

I knew real peace. I knew overwhelming joy. It was the first time I had experienced that.

It is something I never want to lose. I want that for everyone, particularly for teens. I want it for you.

BIBS Is Only a Method

The BIBS method is a simple step-by-step guide on how to know God through His Word. It is not the *only* method of knowing God's Word nor is it the *best* method out there. The *best* method is any method that helps you understand God's Word.

If you follow this book in order and read it cover to cover, you will receive a good method. My dream is that it becomes the best method *for you* as you begin to understand God's Word—perhaps for the first time in your life.

BIBS is just one of many methods, but it has worked well for me and for the teens I am privileged to work with. We used this method with our accompanying daily devotional book, and, from my perspective, it produced a spiritual depth in our teens that they did not have before.

You might not see it in yourself at first, but spiritual progress may be hard to notice when you are in the thick of the fight. Hang in there. Keep going when you are tired. Keep reading your Bible when you do not understand the text. You will get it.

You will never have true peace and joy until you know God intimately, and you will never know God that way without knowing His Word.

Ryan Rench, Youth Director
Calvary Baptist Church, Temecula, CA

PREFACE

I Wish I'd Had This Tool

When I was a teen, I craved something deeper, spiritually. I wanted to know my Bible more, but I did not know how to teach myself. I would *read* the Bible, but I hardly *studied* the Bible. I rarely *meditated* on Scripture. I did not know how. Most of the time, I barely understood what I was reading. "God," I thought, "I'm supposed to *meditate* on your Word?! I'm having a hard time *reading* it!"

Eventually, I became faithful in my Bible reading. I rarely missed a day. It was special to me. My devotions became my favorite time of the day. God became, for the first time in my life, truly real to me.

It was my Junior and Senior year of high school that my craving for spiritual depth began. I needed more.

I would come across these little devotionals—adult and teen editions—and I hated them! They were so shallow! They were so short! They never took *me* deep into Scripture. Maybe the *author* went deep into Scripture himself, but then he wrote down his observations. My devotions amounted to reading his opinions about the Bible rather than leading me into the Bible for myself. I am not a fan of that model.

Candy, Pop and Ice Cream!

My parents used to say, "All you spoiled kids want is candy, pop, and ice cream!" (*Pop* is obviously improper English. Proper grammarians all know the correct word is *soda*.) No child can live a healthy life eating only a "candy, pop and ice cream" diet. Likewise, when devotionals offer only a few verses per day, amounting to about 5 minutes of reading, this little "candy, pop and ice cream snack" of God's Word is no way to live a healthy Christian life.

I finally learned to think for myself. Eventually, I got to where I understood what I was reading, but I had very few tools that would help.

I obediently read and tried to study the Scripture, but if I would have had a book like this at my side, I would have received a lot more from my reading. In some ways, I wasted my growing up years because I never really understood how to read the Bible.

How To Use This Book

My prayer is that Christians can use this as both a **guidebook** and a **reference book** to help them understand what they are reading in their daily devotions.

First, as a **guidebook,** you will learn the BIBS process. Read the *BIBS: Big Idea Bible Study* book from start to finish and get the steps down.

BIBS answers three questions:

- *WHY should I study God's Word?* The Introduction lays out basic principles as to why you should read the Bible.
- *HOW should I study God's Word?* The Observation (Part One) and Interpretation (Part Two) sections show you what to look for in your reading and how to understand what the Bible is saying.
- *WHAT should I do with God's Word?* The Application (Part Three) section drives you to make the Bible personal and make Bible lessons apply to your daily life.

Second, as a **reference book,** BIBS can serve as a long-term tool. Keep it handy. Dog-ear or bookmark the pages that include examples. Highlight the various genres or refer to the step-by-step instructions of interpretation.

Most of all, enjoy! Learn to love your Bible. If you are open enough to God, I promise He will be worth it. Enjoy!

INTRODUCTION

Ideas In

God's Word

CHAPTER 1

KNOWING GOD

THROUGH HIS WORD

One Of My Mentors

Brother Sam Davison was my pastor for the time that I attended Heartland Baptist Bible College in Oklahoma City, OK. He served as the president of the Bible college and taught the weekly homiletics class—a class to train young men how to preach.

No man influenced me more than Brother Sam Davison did in the area of preaching and Bible study. He was an incredible example to me as a man of God.

What made him such an incredible example was not just his

personality or the big church he pastored (around 2,000 members), nor was it his ability to remember names. What made him such a great example to me was his love for the Scriptures.

I have known plenty of pastors and hundreds of people who love God with all their heart, but no one I have ever met has ever loved his or her Bible *more* than Brother Sam Davison. Sure, others might love their Bible *as much,* but no one loves it *more* than him.

I learned from my pastor's example that God's Word has all the answers I will ever need. I learned from him to love and live my Bible. I learned to study my Bible. I learned to hear God's voice every time I open my Bible.

Knowing God Through His Word

I learned how to know God, and I learned that knowing God can only come from knowing His Word.

I know people who would disagree with that last statement. I have heard people say that they can know God through nature. I have heard stories of people meeting God through a vision, dream or some other supernatural experience. I have heard others say that a person cannot know God—that He is unknowable.

However, God is knowable through His Word. I have met Him. He is real to me, and I know hundreds of other people who would say the same thing. I have walked with him and talked with him for several years, and I have a real relationship with him.

"Yes, but how do you *know*?" I have been asked.

The same way I know that I am married. If someone told me, "You're married? You can't know that for sure. You don't even know if your wife is real."

I would respond, "You're crazy! Of course I know she's real! I love my wife. I live with her. I spend time with her. I talk to her and she talks to me. I have a wonderful *relationship* with my wife."

No one will ever be able to make me doubt my relationship with my wife.

The same is true of my relationship with God. He is real. I spend time with Him, and He with me. I love God, and I know He loves me, too. My relationship with Him is real!

Do you know how I spend time with God? Do you know how I have a relationship with Him? You guessed it... through prayer and His Word.

God's Word Is Timeless

Culture changes all the time. The fads of two decades ago are definitely not cool today. New cars get old. The superstars of today are the washed up has-beens of tomorrow.

People need something in their lives that will give them stability. They need an anchor. They need firm ground to stand on. They need something that will not change. They need something that will endure.

Enter God's Word.

God's Word is the anchor that holds all of life together. In a culture that embraces change, almost nothing endures.

The only book that has endured the test of time is the Bible. God wrote it and promised to keep it around forever.

The Bible Is God's Word

The purpose of this book is not to prove the Bible to be true or real. Other authors have devoted their lives to defending (yea, even proving) their belief that the Bible is God's Word (for example, read Josh McDowell's *Evidence that Demands a Verdict* or Robert Sargent's *English Bible: Manuscript Evidence*).

The purpose of this book is to approach the Bible with the full belief that when we open the Bible, we are opening the mind of God. We are hearing His voice when we read the Bible's words. We are reading a perfect book, inspired by God and preserved forever.

> ***Psalm 12:6-7*** *The words of the Lord are pure words: as silver tried in a furnace of earth, purified seven times. Thou shalt keep them, O Lord, thou shalt preserve them from this generation for ever.*

When we open the cover of our Bible, we are receiving revelation from God. He reveals Himself through His Word—the Bible.

Some religions teach that God keeps giving new words through books, visions or modern-day prophets. That is false. He has revealed himself completely through the Bible, and we have all of His revelation that we will ever need.

6

I am passionate about knowing the Bible because it is the basis of everything that is real to me. People can make up dreams and pretend they are from God. People can write new books, magazines or pamphlets and say they are from God, but these new writings have not been proven.

The Bible has been proven. Plenty of times. It has been proven by time, by critics and by cynics. It has been proven by physical attack and skeptical analysis, and it has always won the battles waged against it.

No honest, open-minded person who is seeking truth has ever proven the Bible wrong. Many have tried; all have failed.

Archaeologists keep verifying what Bible-believers have said all along—that Scripture is always accurate. For every new discovery of ancient copies of Scripture, more evidence is piled on the side of the Bible.

A Supernatural Book

The Bible is completely unique, written over a span of hundreds of years, yet somehow unified in its content. Around 40 humans had a part in writing the Bible, yet none of their writings contradict each other.

Without supernatural intervention, the Bible would have been impossible. No other book is like the Bible.

Probabilities and Prophecies

Prophecies of Scripture also verify that it is real—that it is God's Word. Only a fool would deny that Jesus Christ was a real, historical figure (basically every historian agrees that he was a real, living person), yet many people still choose to ignore the prophecies that surround this man, Jesus.

Scores of prophecies were told hundreds of years before Jesus was born. Prophets wrote down their "guesses" as to how this man would live, act and die, and all of their "guesses" came true. Some prophets predicted his birth, some his death. Some predicted his name, some his lineage. Some predicted the timing of his birth, some predicted the place.

All of them were right.

How is that possible? How could a bunch of random guys write a bunch of "random" things about *one person* and they all be right?

Imagine Ben Franklin, George Washington, John Adams, Thomas Jefferson and Paul Revere each sitting at home, writing down random predictions about the presidential elections of 2008, when Barack Obama was first elected as president of the United States.

What if Ben Franklin wrote, "O thou, little Honolulu, from thee cometh the future leader of America." Honolulu was not even part of America yet!

And at another desk, suppose Thomas Jefferson wrote, "He will be president of the United States for two terms."

Suppose George Washington wrote about Barack Obama's wife and two daughters, and suppose several other men wrote about some other aspect of Barack Obama's life.

8

And suppose they were all right.

You would say, "How in the world did they know?! How could they have predicted Honolulu and two terms and two daughters and... That's impossible!"

Of course it is impossible. A bunch of random guys from hundreds of years ago could never have predicted events from the 21st century.

Not Impossible With God

It is impossible for *man*, but not impossible for *God*.

With God, all things are possible. He knows the future.

In fact, when He wrote the Bible, He *did* tell a bunch of "random" guys (His prophets) to write a bunch of "random" predictions (prophecies) about some "future prophet," (Jesus Christ) and all their predictions came true.

Jesus Christ fulfilled dozens of prophecies—a feat that is mathematically impossible. Mathematicians have calculated that for one man to fulfill even *eight* of those prophecies (even though there are at least 61 major prophecies about Christ), the chances are 1 in 100,000,000,000,000,000 (that's 17 zeros!)

If you spread out 100,000,000,000,000,000 silver dollars, it would cover the *entire state of Texas* in a pile 2 feet deep. Now, suppose you mark one of those silver dollars, hide it somewhere in the pile, blindfold a man and tell him to randomly pick any one of those silver dollars.

The chances of him finding your marked silver dollar are 1 in 100,000,000,000,000,000. Those are not great odds.

That figure accounts for only 8 prophecies. The Bible contains hundreds of prophecies.

The math alone is enough to convince me that the Bible is real. By all means, *please* try to prove it wrong! If you can prove those statistics wrong, I will reconsider!

I am so confident (not arrogant) that the Bible is God's Word that I am literally staking my whole life, future and eternity on believing it and living by it.

A Rich, Fulfilled Life

Although mathematics (or, more accurately, *probability*) is not the reason I choose to love God, it certainly validates my faith. I do not have a blind faith. I have a logical, reasonable faith. I have a relationship with God that is as real to me as the 15 inch MacBook Pro I am using to type right now.

God has spoken to me through His Word basically every day since about 8th grade. It was between my 7th and 8th grade years at summer camp when I decided that if God was going to be real to me, I needed to spend time in His Word. Since then, I have not been perfect, but I have regularly read and studied the Bible for myself.

Nothing has changed me and helped me more than getting into the habit of reading my Bible. I am a more disciplined person today because I learned to be disciplined in my devotions when I was in high school. God is blessing my family today because of decisions I made from reading God's Word as a teen. I am living a fulfilled, exciting life today because I chose to let God determine my life's path when I was in junior high.

How About You?

If you are real about serving God, you must be real about His Word.

No one can make you love God. No one can make you love His Word. It has to come from you. There has to be something inside you that cannot be stopped. There has to be a passion inside of you that will keep you going.

Inspiration only lasts so long. You go to Christian summer camp and get fired up from the preaching, but weeks later all that fire is gone. Why?

Why do you lose the fire? Probably because you react to the emotion instead of relying truly on God.

Dave Ramsey says, "Children do what feels good. Adults devise a plan and follow it."

Dave Ramsey says that about your budget. I am saying that about your walk with God. Make a plan to be in His Word.

Are you tired of living off emotions? Are you tired of getting fired up, only to lose the fire a couple weeks later? Are you tired of stinking, spiritually?

If so, then devise a plan and follow it.

God wants you to grow. God wants you to stay fired up. God wants you to be real with Him. God wants a relationship with you.

If you are serious about pleasing God, you must learn to love His Word. That is it. Devise a plan to know God through His Word, and follow that plan.

This Book Is Your Plan

This book is your plan. That is what this book is all about. If you follow the BIBS process, you will learn to hear from God on your own. If you are actively seeking God in His Word, He will speak to you every time.

It will not happen without you. This BIBS Bible study plan is not the magic pill that will get you out of bed every morning—that has to be your choice.

Do not trust this book... trust the Lord. Do not rely on the format... rely on God. I pray this tool is a help to you.

CHAPTER 2

YOU HAVE TO GET IT

Read 5 Minutes

The preacher challenged us, "Read your Bible for at least 5 minutes, every day."

"I can do that," I thought. "5 minutes is easy enough."

In junior high at Christian summer camp, I decided to make Bible reading a priority. I got home from camp on Saturday, crashed on the couch for a couple hours, woke up, had dinner with my family and went right back to bed.

Until Sunday morning. Sunday morning came and I did not read my Bible.

How embarrassing. I had already forgotten my camp decisions.

Just two days prior, at the Friday night campfire I had given a testimony in front of all those people that I was going to read my Bible more, but I already forgot.

Before camp, Sunday mornings were pretty routine: wake up, eat breakfast, get ready for church, go to church, go to lunch, go home, take a nap, wake up, go to church, go home and go to bed. Simple. Routine. It is what I had always done.

Yet the day after getting home from camp, I failed.

Sigh. *This is going to be harder than I thought.*

Remembering To Read

The first hurdle I had to overcome in my Bible reading was actually remembering to read! I knew I should—God had convicted me through the preaching—but it was hard to do. I had to, you know, *work* at it. I had to *try*.

Too bad. So sad. I thought this "5 minutes a day" thing was going to be a breeze, but I failed my first day.

Have you ever been there? Can you relate?

I know people who know that they *should* read the Bible. I have heard testimonies from people, like me, who *committed* to reading their Bible more. In front of everyone they said, "God, I commit to read my Bible at least _____ minutes per day."

I have seen those people fail. Yep, just like me.

It is difficult! I get it! Just *remembering* to read every day is hard. Even if you make a commitment to God—it is still hard!

Understanding What It Says

Remembering to read is hard enough, but we also need to *get it* when we read. If we cannot understand what we are reading, the reading is pointless.

Granted, a certain level of blessing comes from the *discipline* of reading your Bible every day, but the *real* blessing is in the content.

You have to get it

It seems like it should go without saying, but just *reading* your Bible is not the real goal. You should *understand* what you're reading.

For me, getting into the habit of reading my Bible began with a one-year Bible. I would read my section each day as faithfully as I could. When I would miss a day, I would work to catch up, but if I got too far behind, it seemed hopeless. Too many pages.

Then, when I would get all inspired to catch up, I would end up speed-reading (actually skimming). The problem was, I did not understand any of it.

Even when I was reading faithfully each day and rarely missing a day (into my high school years), I still would not fully understand what I was reading. I would read, yes, but it only helped me a little.

At times it felt like homework. It felt like required reading. It felt like a textbook.

I would catch a verse here or there or I would see an old sermon note that would provide an outline of what I was reading, but I could never really step back and see the big picture. I never saw the Bible as a book. I always saw it as a collection of verses.

Novels

I was a reader in high school. I used to read for fun. I read several Frank Peretti books, the *Indian in the Cupboard* series, a few of the *Horatio Hornblower* series, some Nancy Drew and Hardy Boys mysteries, all of Bro. Ed Dunlop's books and more.

When I read novels, I knew what I was reading. I would start at the beginning, follow the author's storyline as the plot unfolded, and reach the climax with the author. I would conclude each chapter or section understanding what the author said.

Reading my Bible was different, though. When I read my Bible, I treated it like a different kind of book. Instead of looking at it like a novel in which the author has a flow of thought, I treated it like I had always treated the Bible: I opened it to a verse and just started reading.

Wait a minute... do we ever do that with a novel? Do you walk up to a bookshelf, pick up a novel, open up to page 72 and just start reading in the middle of a paragraph?

No.

You read a novel a certain way. You follow the author's flow of thought. You experience the story as he writes it. As you turn page by page, you get more and more information. When you find yourself at page 103, you can think back to the details and plot twists from the previous pages.

In this book, as you learn the BIBS format, you will learn to approach the Bible the same way you approach a novel—getting inside the author's head and experiencing the book as it was written.

When you understand what you are reading, the Bible moves from "required" reading to pleasure reading. Fiction novels are pleasurable. The Bible can be too.

CHAPTER 3

WHY "BIBS?"

Big Idea Bible Study

You might think, "So why is it called *BIBS?* How insulting! Do you think we are babies?!"

Don't get mad. You are not a baby.

B.I.B.S. is just an acronym. Each letter stands for a word: Big Idea Bible Study. The BIBS format is a simple way to study your Bible.

The idea is this: you read a text (usually just a few verses), then you work to figure out what God is saying in *that* text. The human author had something he was trying to say. God used *that* human author to write *that* text at *that* time to *those* people for *that* purpose.

What purpose? That is your job—figure it out.

Work at finding the Big Idea (BIBS), or the intent, of the biblical author. At this point, you will not need to worry about cross-references or side-by-side comparison Bibles. Just read *that* text and find God's intent through that one author.

Author's Intent

Too many people get hung up on cross-references and lose sight of God's message at a particular time. God said something originally in the gospel of John to a certain group of people. He also said something different in the gospel of Luke to another group of people. Sure, John and Luke might tell some of the same stories, but the intent of the authors is different.

Matthew wrote some of the same stories as Mark, but God's intent is not necessarily that we get ALL the details from ALL the gospels. God's intent is that we get a *message* from His Word. He used John to present a *message* to a certain group of people, and then he used Luke to tell the same story but present an entirely different *message* to a different group of people.

Just because Scripture is perfectly unified in its content, we should not take that to mean that it all has to crisscross and interweave like spaghetti. Yes, the Bible is a cohesive unit and every passage works in harmony with the other passages, but it is not imperative to cross reference every text in order to properly understand it. Else, what would the text have meant before the cross reference was written?

"You Did It All Wrong!"

The man stormed up to me after I had finished preaching. His voice was flushed with adrenaline. "You did it all wrong! You completely missed the point! You did not preach that right at all. You are preaching this text like we are some kind of bad people, when it clearly says in the cross reference of my John MacArthur Bible that Paul told Timothy it's the devil's pressures that make us unfaithful!"

He had one of those Bibles with the little letters and numbers that referred you to the center column. There you would find other Bible references that were loosely along the same topic or that had similar ideas.

Apparently, the verse in Proverbs that I preached had a little reference letter that linked that verse to another topic in 1 Timothy. This man took that to mean that MacArthur's reference was more important than the clarity of the verse itself!

I like reference Bibles. I have a few, and I use them now and then.

But Mr. MacArthur's references are not inspired. Mr. MacArthur is not God, nor does he claim to be. Therefore, Mr. MacArthur's references (or Scofield, Thompson Chain or any other references) are not Bible truth... the Bible is Bible truth!

When the man who spoke with me followed the cross-reference from the Proverb to the New Testament, he found a completely different meaning to the text I had preached. The Proverb took on a completely new interpretation based on the verse in 1 Timothy.

I have to wonder sarcastically (shame on me)... what did the Proverb mean for the hundreds of years before Paul wrote 1 Timothy? What did Solomon mean when he originally wrote the

Proverb? Was God hiding the message until Paul could come around later and clear it up?

No. This Proverb was not a type or an allegory. It was not a hidden secret verse with deep theological insights that could only be unlocked thousands of years later by scholars with cross-reference Bibles.

The Proverb meant something to its original readers. By finding Solomon's intent, we find God's intent. By finding God's intent, we hear God's voice.

God's Revelation

God spoke in the past to people's problems. He fixed the mess of sin by making His will known to man. Man wrote it down, little by little, in various books. These books were protected and copied, and ultimately compiled into what we call the Holy Bible.

God spoke and men wrote what God told them to write. The more God wrote, the less He had to speak, because He had already spoken.

God spoke directly with Adam, the first man. Moses was the leader who wrote the law based on God's revelation to him. The Old Testament prophets preached to God's people, then wrote the messages down. By the end of the Old Testament, history books, law books, song books, wisdom books and more were what comprised God's Word to mankind.

God had spoken, and men wrote it down.

A few hundred years passed and then Jesus was born as the Messiah. He amassed a following and introduced a radical new idea—the Gospel. Jesus' disciples told the story of Christ as God inspired them to write. Other followers of Christ, like Paul the apostle, became missionaries and church planters, and followed up their mission works with letters written back to the churches, church members and pastors.

God spoke to all mankind through these accounts and letters.

Man's job got simpler and simpler... find a copy of these letters, read them, and obey them!

The hard part was compiling the letters. It took several decades, but finally the Scriptures were gathered (so to speak) from all over the world and compiled into one book—the Bible.

God revealed His mind to man little by little—over hundreds of years. While His *method* might be different today than it was when He spoke to Adam, His desire is still the same—that we hear His voice and obey Him!

It really is that simple.

Obeying the Bible will put us in God's will all the time. No matter what.

Do you want to be right with God? Then search the Scriptures, hear God's voice, and obey Him.

You do not need a bunch of fancy books or a bunch of scholars telling you what to do. Just search the Scripture for yourself, study a particular text, understand what it said originally, and then apply it to yourself. That is how God speaks to you today.

So, Why the "Big Idea?"

If God speaks through His Word today, and our job is to study out a particular text and hear His voice, what is all this fuss about a "Big Idea?"

Even the title of this book talks about the Big Idea. What is the idea behind this "Big Idea?"

Every Note Has a Big Idea

Every note you write has some sort of Big Idea (or author intent). You learned the various formats of letters when you were in elementary school, right? Friendly letters and business letters have different formats and are intended for different purposes.

A **thank-you card** has a specific intent: thanking someone for something.

A **letter of recommendation** has a specific intent: recommending someone or something.

A **love letter** has a specific and single intent. Are you seeing the pattern? What do you suppose the intent of a love letter is? Wishing someone a happy birthday? Of course not!

When you sit to write any kind of note or draft some sort of business letter, there is almost always a specific and single reason. Letters and notes often basically say only one thing: "Thank you," "I recommend...," or "I love you." for example. The body of the letter has lots to say, but as a whole, it only says one thing.

The Bible Has Big Ideas

Biblical authors were no different from authors today. Just like a novelist carries a thought through his novel, the biblical author also conveys a big thought through his book. Just as a friendly letter to your cousin is intended to cheer him up after hearing of his job loss, the biblical author might send a note to encourage his friend to love others (Philemon).

Every book of the Bible has a major theme. Do not approach the Bible as if it is a bunch of unrelated thoughts. Do not think of the Bible like it is just a bunch of verses clumped together.

Think of the Bible as a book. It is a book of books, and each of the 66 books has a major theme of its own.

Further, each book is broken down into smaller ideas, and those ideas can be broken down into even smaller ideas.

For example, the book of Romans is one of the 66 books of the Bible. My pastor in college, Bro. Sam Davison, preached through Romans and called the series, "Romans: The Pure Gospel." He repeatedly brought each sermon to the Gospel—the message of the death, burial and resurrection of Jesus Christ as a means to forgive sin and change our lives.

That was the main theme: "The Pure Gospel." It was the Big Idea of the book.

However, we can break Romans down even further. Just like the various parts of this BIBS book are broken down into other Big Ideas (Introduction, Part One, Part Two, etc.), we can further break the book of Romans into parts:

- **Condemnation** (chapters 1-3 show God's condemnation of all mankind's sin.)
- **Salvation** (chapters 3-5 explain Christ's payment for our sin.)
- **Sanctification** (chapters 6-8 explain how Christians can live in the Holy Spirit's power.)
- **Dispensation** (chapters 9-11 explain Israel's continued role in the Gospel message.)
- **Application** (chapters 12-16 teach Christians how to act in light of their salvation.)

Each part of Romans is several chapters long, yet it contains a Big Idea.

We can further break each part of Romans down into whole chapters, and each chapter can be split even further into smaller texts.

When you attend church and the pastor reads the text for his sermon, he typically reads about 4 or 5 verses, prays, and then says, "Today we are going to talk about the family..." or "Today's topic is how to love God..." or "The title of my sermon is how to overcome temptation."

He gives the text, and then he gives the Big Idea.

Sometimes the sermon has several stories, illustrations, examples or explanations included, but usually the sermon is about one thing. A preacher cannot preach the entire Bible every single week. He has to pace himself!

One Idea

The preacher shoots for one idea in his sermon. Several supporting ideas come into play, but his goal is singular. He is after the Big Idea of the text.

He is trying to figure out what God said originally, and what God, through the Bible, is still saying to us today. The preacher's job is to bring timeless truth to today's world. His job requires that he studies the text, finds the Big Idea, and then presents that idea in a way that will help the hearer improve his or her life in some way.

This one idea that the preacher searches for is the same idea you should search for every day in your own personal devotions. If the preacher should do it, why not you? If God thinks it is helpful for a congregation to understand His Word through *preaching*, why not through your own *study*, too?

We see Big Ideas everywhere:

Debate. If you are involved in a debate class, you have a team line, right? You know your core arguments and you are prepared to beat the other team with your one main argument by repeating it as often as possible. You have other supporting materials and counter-arguments, but your team line is most important. It sums up your whole side of the debate. It is your Big Idea.

Advertising. Advertisers know that in order for their product to make sense, they have to boil their product down to a Big Idea. When Apple first introduced the iPod, the Big Idea of their advertisements was the iPod slogan: "1,000 songs in your pocket." Did the slogan say everything about Apple? No. Did it explain how the iPod worked? No. Did it give all the details of the color and design? No. The Big Idea of the iPod condensed an entire product line into one neat little phrase.

Journalism. Open any newspaper and the first sentence of almost every article is called *the lead*. The lead is a sentence or two that sums up the whole article and gives the most important information right up front. The lead is the journalist's Big Idea; the rest of the details of the story follow.

Mission Statement. Most businesses, institutions and even families will work to craft a mission statement—a sentence or two that summarizes and guides the decisions and actions of the institution. A family's mission statement might be something as simple as, "We exist to bring glory to God." A Christian school might craft everything they do with the goal of "producing committed followers of Jesus Christ."

Dave Ramsey runs a company of 400 employees, a national radio show, a counseling center, an education center devoted to churches, military, public schools, businesses and more. He is an author, a radio personality, a national voice for Christ as well as a husband and dad. He runs the publications arm, the media arm, the education arm, the philosophy arm and every other arm in his company. Dave Ramsey's company has so many arms it looks like a creature from Disney's *Monsters Inc.* Dave Ramsey is able to stay on course with this one summarizing mission statement: *The Lampo Group, Inc. is providing biblically based, common sense education and empowerment which gives HOPE to everyone from the financially secure to the financially distressed.* Now that is one Big Idea!

Old Testament. In the Old Testament, the prophets would often communicate the "Burden of the Lord." They would preach sermons that would span several printed pages in our Bible, but the sermon would still contain a single unifying thought.

All Scripture. No matter where you look in Scripture, the verse you read will be part of a bigger idea. It might have a single Big

Idea within the verse itself, but it will also have a bigger idea within the chapter and the book, as well.

Our job as Christians is to find the Big Idea of what God is trying to say. He does not speak merely a verse at a time. He speaks in ideas. He speaks in chunks of thought.

Each section of Scripture (we call it a *passage* or *text*) will contain truth that can be summed up in a simpler statement. God speaks to us in principles far more than specifics.

The principle of a text might be, "Love your neighbor like you love yourself." The specific truth is that you should love your parents, your annoying little brother, that jerk in your class, the bully in PE, the President of the United States and that girl who lied about you last week. God is speaking to you in principles; you have to know how to hear Him in the specifics.

Learn to find Big Ideas in every text you read.

Deep and wide

Bible study is both deep and wide. Sometimes people get lost in the depths of Scripture. At other times they breeze so quickly through the chapters that they miss the gold nuggets along the way.

To me, the best times in my life are when I am deep in God's Word.

However, I cannot truly get deeper into a biblical text until I have read several chapters before and after it. I need to jump into the biblical author's river of thought.

Bible study needs both—both the depths of the text and the full context (or flow) of the biblical author's thoughts.

So?

The Big Idea Bible Study (BIBS) is designed to be both an **in-depth** look at certain portions of Scripture as well as a **birds-eye view** of the biblical text.

Further, with BIBS we desire to analyze certain portions of Scripture to see:

- What the original intent was
- What the timeless truth is
- What it means for us today

Observation, Interpretation, Application

Our goal as Christians is to find God's will and obey it. The way we find His will is through His Word. As long as we are clear on what His Word says, we will be clear about His will.

Each passage in Scripture will have one interpretation that is right, but several applications of the principle to influence how we live today.

One interpretation. Multiple applications.

The Bible *said* one thing. Find out what it *said*, and you will then be able to find out what it is *saying* still today.

We will borrow the structure set by Howard Hendricks in his book *Living By the Book* as we go through his three main steps:

- **Observation** – The birds-eye view.
- **Interpretation** – What is God saying?
- **Application** – What is God saying *to me*?

PART ONE

OBSERVATION

CHAPTER 4

OBSERVATION - THE

BIRDS-EYE VIEW

A Trip To the Library

You walk into a library and plan on reading a book. Even *before* picking up the novel, you scan the library for what shelf to start looking. You see signs hanging from the ceiling: Non-Fiction, Periodicals, Children's Books...

You are drawn to the kids' section but have to keep scanning.

Ah! There it is! The fiction section.

Already, you have an idea of what type of book you will be reading.

Fiction. It will be a story. It will not be a reference book, a poetry book or a school book. It will be an entertainment book.

As you walk toward the fiction section, you hone in on the shelf you typically read from. Science Fiction. (You nerd!)

You browse the Astro-Galactic-Fighter-Spaceship-Mega-Alien Series for the next one in the lineup. Right at eye level, you scan the spines for the right title.

"There you are!" you think to yourself. You reach up for *The Battle of the Mega-Galactic-Alien-Invaders: The Glonkin Tribe Returns* and pull it off the shelf.

You glance over the front cover and notice the author's name at the bottom center. You see the title and think, "That's a weirdly long title, but it pretty much tells me what the book is going to be about." You notice the graphics. The dark black background implies outer space, and the bright green and blue lettering indicate the laser-gun battles that are to come.

You flip the book over and read the summary on the back cover. You get the gist of what the book will be about. You read the author's biography and see what type of a person he is.

Before opening the book, you have a good idea of what direction it will take.

You walked to the fiction section. You browsed the science fiction shelf. You found the particular series and book. You scanned the front cover and read the back cover.

You know the genre and the author. You know the setting, the mindset, and the people in the story line. You have read other books in the series, so you have an idea of the history of the book's characters.

Guess what? The way you approach a novel is the same way you should approach the Bible. What you do every time you browse the library for a novel is what we will call *Observation*.

Observation

Think about the library trip again. You did not blindly walk up to a random shelf, pick out a random book you knew nothing about, and start reading in the middle of the chapter.

Yet we do this with the Bible all the time... at least I did.

I would open my Bible, look for a verse I had marked in church or memorized in AWANA and start reading.

I never *observed*.

What is Observation?

You may wonder, "What is observation?"

Observation is what I like to call the "birds-eye view." Before diving into the book, take a look at the broad picture. Fly up into the sky and view the text from above. Before starting at the introduction and chapter 1, start with the author and genre instead.

In our library analogy, picture yourself walking into the library front doors. You are looking across the aisles of books. At the end of each shelf is a sign that tells what genre—or type of literature—each book on that shelf is.

Ask some broad questions in your observation of the Bible text:

- Why was the book written in the first place?
- What happened in this story before this text?
- To whom is it written?
- What is the problem with mankind that God is trying to fix with this text? (It has to address some need... what is it?)
- What type (or genre) of writing is it?

Observation is a simple step back. It is a survey. It is the background information. It is the width before we get into the depth. It is the big, Big Idea—the ultra-super-Big Idea.

Do Not Skip Observation

Please do not skip this step! Too often, we dive right into a text when we have never taken the time to observe. Observation helps keep us from error. It keeps us from reading things *into* the text rather than getting things *out of* what is plainly there.

Did you know that the Bible includes lies? Yep. It does.

Before you get confused or mad, remember that the Bible records everything perfectly, including the lies of Satan. When Satan speaks, the Bible records his words, even when they are lies. Observation helps you step back from your reading and say, "Wait, who said this?"

We get into trouble when we "cherry-pick" our favorite verses out of Scripture. For example, you might have heard the (fake) story of the guy who was frantically searching for God's will, so he flipped open his Bible, pointed to a random verse and started reading how Judas "went and hanged himself" (Matthew 27:5). Scary! He flipped several more pages and read Jesus' words in red: "Go and do thou likewise." (Luke 10:37) The man thinks, *"Wait, WHAT?! This can't be right!"* So he flips the pages again and reads, "That thou doest, do quickly." (John 13:27)

No, that is not a true story. And no, that is not how God leads.

If this man had observed, or gotten the bigger picture, he would have understood those verses.

Before diving into a verse, look at the context. Observe the whole letter. Step back from the *one phrase* you are stuck on. Instead of building an entire theology on a snapshot, study the whole scene.

Misusing Scripture

To insert your own theology into a text is to put words in God's mouth. He has not hidden his Word. He has no deep secrets that He reveals only to the smartest people.

People who study numbers, patterns and figures in the Bible often go so deep that they miss the plain truth of Scripture. If you look hard enough, you can find practically anything in Scripture. For example, Shakespeare is "in the Bible" because the 46th word from the beginning of Psalm 46 (KJV) is *shake* and the 46th word from the end of the Psalm (not counting *Selah*) is *spear*. People read that and say, "See! Shakespeare's in the Bible!" Don't be crazy.

Just read the Bible and stop trying to use it as your little secret codebook.

People named Mark might like Psalm 37:37, "Mark the perfect man," but is God really saying that people named *Mark* are perfect? Nope.

"Try the spirits" in 1 John 4:1 is *not* God's approval on drinking alcohol (spirits). Read the whole context to find out what God is communicating.

Study the Bible like it is a letter with a specific intent of the author. The details might seem like a rabbit trail, but the author has an overall goal. He has a Big Idea. Find that Big Idea first.

If you lift a verse out of context, without observation, you could look like a fool. Ignoring observation is like lifting choice words out of a letter. You might get an entirely different outcome!

Dear Darla, I hate your stinkin' guts. You make me vomit. You're scum between my toes. Love, Alfalfa.

If Alfalfa had really sent that letter to Darla, do you think she would have read that and said, "Oh how sweet! Alfalfa wants me to love him because he put the word *love* in there!"

No way! She would have punched him in the face.

You open a letter from your landlord:

Dear Mr. and Mrs. John Smith, This letter is to inform you that unless you pay your bill, you will be forcibly removed from the premises. You have 5 days before you are evicted. Have a nice day.

You would not read that and say, "Oh how nice. They want me to have a nice day."

Just like the eviction notice has one point (get out of the house), so too does a book of the Bible have one point. Do not cherry-pick verses. Read the whole letter. Just like the eviction notice, ask, "What is the point of this letter?"

Here is a hint... the eviction notice's Big Idea is *not*, "Have a nice day." Do not forget to observe.

CHAPTER 5

WAYS TO OBSERVE

Birds-Eye View

A bird has a lot to look at when he is up in the sky. He looks at the trees for a place to nest. He scans the ground for a bug to snatch. He looks up for predators, out for distance, around for scenery, back for recall, or down for rest.

Depending on what the bird needs, his view can go in several directions.

Just as a bird has a broad perspective, observation will take a broad search of topics. When we observe a Bible text, we, too, have several directions we can look. Observation includes several key areas including genre, author, background, theme and more.

Genre

Each genre will have a different twist to it. You know this from common experience.

Letters. Take different types of letters, for example. When you go to your mailbox you will see different types of mail: junk mail, business mail, personal mail, etc. If you notice a bill from Verizon, you read it differently than a note from Grandma talking about your cousins that live near her. If you receive a business letter from ABC Company Inc., you will read it differently from a love letter. A thank you note is different from an advertisement. You get the idea.

Music. You instinctively know that different genres of music create different moods and feelings. You do not play big, loud, bubbly circus music during the intense graveyard scene of a horror movie. That is the wrong genre. Similarly, you would not play creepy horror music in its eerie minor key if you were showing a scene of happy little babies laughing and playing together.

Literature. Each genre of music is interpreted differently; the same is true in literature.

Different types of reading materials mean that you automatically think of them differently. You read poems differently than textbooks. You read *Hamlet* differently than you read text messages. You read research material for your class debate differently than a note from your youth pastor.

In the Bible, each genre is different, and has its own rules of how to read it.

For a more in-depth look at various genres—where they are found, how to read them, what to look for, etc.—please see Appendix 1 in the back of this book. Here is an overview of some of the genres found in Scripture:

The Basic Genres

- **History or Narrative**: These are stories found in Genesis, Exodus, Numbers, Joshua, Judges, Ruth, 1 and 2 Samuel, 1 and 2 Kings, 1 and 2 Chronicles, Ezra, Nehemiah, Esther, Jonah and Acts. Narratives often give one broad story with a central idea—something we might call a *moral* as in *Aesop's Fables*. Narratives can be taken as a whole (sometimes several chapters long) or broken into smaller sections.
- **Law**: The Law is a collection of God's laws for His people, particularly under Moses' leadership. The Law includes Leviticus and Deuteronomy, as well as other texts.
- **Wisdom**: Wisdom is simple axioms, catchy truths and deep thoughts from life such as Job, Proverbs and Ecclesiastes.
- **Poetry**: These are the prose and rhymes such as Psalms, Song of Solomon and Lamentations. Poetry was often used to express emotions through poems or songs. They usually include one unified thought comprised of many smaller ideas.
- **Prophecy**: These include both major and minor prophets such as Isaiah, Jeremiah, Ezekiel, Daniel, Hosea, Joel, Amos, Obadiah, Micah, Nahum, Habakkuk, Zephaniah, Haggai, Zechariah and Malachi. The prophets spoke on God's behalf, often calling people to repentance. While

their message was specific to a nation, their truth still applies to us today.

- **Apocalyptic**: These are combinations of narrative and prose written in vivid imagery and poetic phrases. Careful study is needed to interpret these passages, but they are not meant to intimidate the reader into thinking all is fake. Unless it is expressly allegorical (where words represent other meanings), we interpret the Bible literally and believe that events will happen as they are described. Much Apocalyptic writing is found in Daniel and Revelation.
- **Parable**: These are the sayings of Jesus that are narrative and instructional, contained in the Gospels. The meaning of the parable is often found in the context of the chapter. For example, the parable might be a story that Jesus tells in order to answer someone's question.
- **Epistle**: These are the letters written to a specific audience that are practical for us today such as Romans, 1 and 2 Corinthians, Galatians, Ephesians, Philippians, Colossians, 1 and 2 Thessalonians, 1 and 2 Timothy, Titus, Philemon, Hebrews, James, 1 and 2 Peter, John (the three epistles) and the first three chapters of Revelation. Epistles were written to churches or individuals and are usually quite straightforward. You read an epistle as you do any letter— as a complete unit.
- **Romance**: These are narrative, written also as love stories, such as Ruth and Song of Solomon. Within romance writings are timeless truths that affect us today.

Before ever diving into how to get something out of your Bible reading, you have to first make sure that you are not misunderstanding the genre. Is the author using poetic language to make a point? Is it a picture, or is it to be taken literally? Is it a narrative story, setting up the scene for the big punch at the end, or does *every* detail have some kind of spiritual significance?

These are some questions you can ask when you are first starting to study a passage.

Author

Who is the author?

The Holy Spirit is the author, of course, but He couched His words in the life, style of writing, and experiences of the human author.

> **2 Peter 1:20-21** *Knowing this first, that no prophecy of the scripture is of any private interpretation. For the prophecy came not in old time by the will of man: but holy men of God spake as they were moved by the Holy Ghost.*

Each human author had his own experiences and expertise. David was a musician, so he wrote several songs (Psalms). Paul was a devoted theologian before being saved, so God used Paul's expertise in the law to write doctrine-heavy letters.

Each author is unique and originally had some reason to write. Something was going on in the world that required God's voice. Holy men of God wrote what the Holy Spirit told them, but these men were not being mindless robots. They were not blindly writing like zombies.

Reading Paul's letters will prove that he is no robot. To the church in Corinth—a sin-filled church that was becoming anti-Paul—the apostle wrote scathing rebukes and taught clear doctrine. To the church in Thessalonica—a baby church he spent very little time with—Paul loved them "as a nurse cherisheth her children" (1 Thessalonians 2:7) and "exhorted and comforted and charged every one of you, as a father doth his children." (1 Thessalonians 2:11)

Knowing the human author will help to humanize the people in the Bible. Instead of thinking of them as Bible characters—a term we might associate with actors in a movie or characters in a fiction novel—think of them as real, live human beings, just like you. Paul struggled with anger, fear and lying, just like you. David had lustful thoughts. John got jealous. Peter worried about his self-image. Ezekiel, I am sure, was uncomfortable with his message from God—he did not want to look like a lunatic. Even Jesus himself was human and was tempted exactly in the same way we are tempted, yet without sin. (Hebrews 4:15)

Do not make the Bible mystical or mythological. Bible stories are not at all the same as stories about Hercules, Zeus and Venus. Bible stories are real. They are true historical accounts. They are real events that happened to real people.

Get to know the author. You might discover why God wrote that particular book. If you can figure out what God *said* in the past, you will be well on your way to figuring out what God is *saying* in the present.

Background

During Bible college, every Sunday night was fun. I looked forward to the preaching. Pastor Sam Davison was in a series called "Exciting Stories from the Kings and Prophets," recounting the stories from the Old Testament and bringing the timeless principles to today's world.

The most intriguing part of each sermon was the background information. Pastor Davison would start with the Scripture reading, tell a simple story as his introduction, and then back up about 6 chapters and retell the previous weeks' sermons.

He would not go into the same level of detail as he went in the weeks prior, but he would always spend ample time (sometimes up to 20 or 30 minutes) on background.

Why? What's the big deal, right?

Here is why: Pastor Davison provided background detail so that the congregation could understand the Bible. Simple.

David, Solomon, Hezekiah, Isaiah, Daniel and all the other kings and prophets did not live in isolation. The kings of the Old Testament did not start their own country each time they ruled. The prophets did not preach to any random nation they chose.

The kings were always part of some sort of royal family. Turmoil surrounded almost every change of throne. Sin filled the nations, so the prophet's job was never done.

Each new king that reigned was inheriting a mess. Sometimes the Bible describes a king's reign in one verse. Other kings were subjects of far more detail. All the kings, though, were part of something much bigger than themselves.

The nation of Israel has a storied past that traces all the way to Abraham the forefather. The incredible journey of Israel's history includes deceit, treachery, miracles, slavery, deliverance, testing, arrogance, victory and defeat. The Jewish people went from being led directly by God to being delivered by judges, guided by prophets and controlled by kings.

Israel's history is just one example of how background information is necessary to understand a text. For someone to dive headlong into the present (i.e. reading the story of David and Goliath), he must first understand the past (i.e. how Israel got to the point where David had to fight Goliath).

Each movement of a story is part of a bigger picture, like a scene of a play is part of the bigger act. The biblical author wrote the story of Daniel in the lion's den, for example, in light of Daniel's entire life. Daniel did not wake up one day and decide to obey God. He had obeyed God as a boy at home, as a teen in the palace, and as second ruler to three world dictators. His walk with God did not begin in the lion's den as an old man. His walk with God began as a boy and continued through his entire life.

Background information tells the reader what has happened in the past. Every person has a story. Every story has a past. Every past is interesting and adds understanding to the present.

The background information of a biblical passage may be as simple as reading the previous few verses to know what is going on. Your research may be as extensive as a deep study of the whole book.

At least do something. Do SOME research. At least read something about the past before diving headlong into the present.

No text lives in isolation. Each is part of something bigger.

Step back. Fly up a little higher and take in the broader picture. You will be glad you did.

Information To Look For

You think, "Background information, huh? What in the world do I look for?!" I am glad you asked.

Dates. First, get an idea of the date of writing. Is it the Old or New Testament? Is it the time of Christ, early church or the time of Israel's kings? Is it before or after Moses? Before or after the flood? Are there prophets, judges or kings?

Get your bearings in Scripture. You can reference charts or graphs that show the main movements of Scripture with key Bible characters like Adam, Abraham, Joseph, Moses, David, Jesus, Paul and others. You should have an understanding of how God moved through time.

Although God's *nature* is unchanging, His *methods* have changed. He speaks to us differently today than He did in the Old Testament. We live in an entirely new era and under a completely new set of rules and expectations.

Knowing the date of the writing is the first key to look for in your background check of Scripture.

Occasion of Writing. Not only will the date be a key factor in understanding the text, but the occasion of writing will help, as well. Figure out why the text needed to be written in the first place. Why is it there? Whom is God trying to help? Why did the author need to write it at that time? What is the sin that God is correcting? What is the thinking problem that God is fixing? What is the error that God is fighting? What is the issue that God is addressing?

The occasion of the writing brings purpose to the text. Each text in the Bible was written on purpose. It had meaning and value for a particular people at a particular time. Knowing the past purpose will help us understand the Bible's present purpose.

Since mankind's problems are the same today as they have always been—the world, the flesh and the devil—God's answers are always the same. His answers are in His Word. Knowing the original struggle will help us relate to our current struggle. Knowing the original answer will give us today's answer too.

Culture. What is the culture of the people to whom the biblical author is writing? Understanding the original readers' culture will help you understand why certain topics were covered in Scripture. While we today might not have as much direct application to our lives, we can better understand the principle by understanding the original culture.

For example, understanding a little about the city and people of Corinth will help us understand why so many problems existed in the church there. Corinth was a coastal city filled with merchants of all kinds. About half the city's inhabitants were rich business people and the other half were slaves or former slaves. The money that poured through the city led to sin of all kinds, including idolatry and sexual immorality—sins prominent in the church there, as well. Paul wrote two letters to the Corinthian church to set their sin in order.

We might be shocked or horrified at the Corinthian church's sin unless we understood what they were surrounded with. We might think we could never relate to their horrible sin until we start to consider the same principles of our own horrible sin, too.

Knowing the Corinthian culture—or, for that matter, Israel's, Nineveh's, Jerusalem's or Rome's—will help us relate to our own culture and the other cultures of today.

The Bible is a timeless book that has applied to every culture throughout all of time. God's Word to the original readers was the same Word to people in the Dark Ages, the Babylonian Empire, America's Civil War, the Ming Dynasty and everything in between. Cultures have drastically changed, but sin is always the same. God's Word has remained timeless—true to all cultures of all time.

Theme. Part of your background check might include a quick scan of the overall themes of a book. Again, some themes might apply more directly than others, but all will be beneficial to you in some way.

Find the overall movements of the text and discover what the chapter is about. If you have dug into the author, the culture, the date and other background information, chances are high that you have uncovered certain themes.

Is the original reader part of an idolatrous culture? The theme will probably include something against idolatry. Is the culture full of sexual sin? Expect a theme about purity.

Themes may broadly cover the whole book. Esther is a book with the running theme of God's sovereignty. Sovereignty is written into every page and in every event of Esther's life. The main theme is seen all throughout the book.

At other times, the theme might not be so obvious. Or, the theme might not be as deep into each page. The book of Romans covers many different themes. So does Genesis.

Each book uniquely covers various themes. Find the overall theme in the background information before diving deep into a Scriptural text.

Tools of the Trade

Start With Your Toothbrush. Some tools—dentist drills, for example—are used only by specialists. I would not recommend drilling out your own cavities.

However, other tools—toothbrushes, for example—are for everyone. I do recommend you use a toothbrush daily. Do not leave your teeth cleaning up to your dentist. Your annual checkup does not count as good hygiene. Use the tools you have.

A specialist's tools might do incredible work, but only the specialist knows how to use them. Sure, anyone can learn dentistry over time, but it makes sense for everyone to just start with a toothbrush.

If you are a Christian, you do not have to be a specialist—like a pastor, missionary, evangelist, or other kind of minister—to use the tool of God's Word. Use your "toothbrush." Know the basics of Bible study and you will have a great head start.

Personal hygiene does not happen at the annual cleaning; it happens in the day-to-day brushing. Personal hygiene is incremental—a little bit every day.

The same is true with your Christian walk with God. A Bible specialist's tools—a huge library, fancy Bible software, etc.—will not make sense to you if you are a beginner. Start simple, and grow incrementally.

The following are a few tools that you might already have:

Study Bible. A study Bible will give you an overview of the book before you begin reading. The overview might include several of the points previously mentioned including background information, date, author, themes and cultural references. Further, the Bible might include cross references, maps and further explanations as you are reading through a text.

Concordance. A concordance such as *Strong's Exhaustive Concordance* will allow you to look up any word in the Bible and see the reference to *every* verse that word is in. In addition, it will define the word in its original language. This resource is helpful to see how ideas relate to one another and how words are defined within a context.

Online Bibles. Concordances and other reference materials are available free online. Advantages include speed and availability. Examples of online sources include classic.net.bible.org or blueletterbible.org. Each website (and several others like them) allows you to click on a word to view the definition and uses within Scripture.

Bible Software. If you prefer to download software, consider www.e-sword.net as a free option. Good dictionaries such as Webster's 1828 can be downloaded for free through E-Sword, as well as several commentaries, maps, devotionals and more. On my Mac I use the Olive Tree Bible App and purchase study books that sync with my iPad and iPhone. I have access to hundreds of resources and use them almost daily.

Books. Other people have out-studied you, so glean from their brains. You can do this through books. I love hearing from men and women who are smarter than me. I listen to a lot of what they tell me through their books. I gain a lot of background information about the Bible when I read after people who have devoted their lives to other languages, cultures and histories. I do not have time to become an archaeologist, so I read about archaeologist's findings. I do not have time to become a historian with a focus on the Babylonian Empire, so when I am studying Daniel (who lived during the Babylonian Empire), I read what the experts wrote.

Survey books such as Bible handbooks, Bible atlases, and Bible dictionaries will help you understand cultures, people and other background information. Whole-Bible commentaries such as *King James Bible Commentary* will not only provide an overview of each book but will also explain trouble sections through the Bible. Commentaries are volumes dedicated to each book of the Bible. A complete commentary will deal in depth with every word and phrase of every verse of the Bible.

Your Pastor. Your pastor has a spiritual calling as a man of God. He is placed in your life to help you. He is a specialist, so to speak, and he has plenty of tools to help you. Ask him if you can see his library. If he allows, ask him if you can borrow books. Get his recommendations on what books to study. If you are studying Romans, see if he has any background or survey books available. If you are doing a topical study on purity, see if he has any books on that topic.

Warning! Use man's wisdom sparingly! Your goal is to hear from God directly, so do not rely on these Bible study tools as a crutch. You are not after the right answer, as if you are taking a test in school. You are hearing from God, so spend most of your time in His Word! Books, commentaries, concordances, articles and your Pastor are fallible—they have errors. God is infallible. His Word is inerrant. Man's writings (including this book you are reading right now) are filled with error. God is perfect, so trust God more than men.

PART TWO

INTERPRETATION

CHAPTER 6

INTERPRETATION - WHAT IS GOD SAYING?

Big, Scary Words

Sometimes teens like to play dumb, and they pretend to be scared of big words. They have joked around with academics their whole lives and have never been serious about learning. They are not dumb, but they pretend to be.

I do not know why people pretend to be dumb. Most of the teens that I know are quite intelligent. They understand big, scary words (so called), and they can grasp deep concepts.

Yet some people joke about big, scary words and pretend they do not know what they mean. The crazy thing is that almost all of us carry around a really smart device that can act like a dictionary if we want it to—our phones!

Big, scary words do not have to be big or scary.

If you are one who plays dumb, sharpen your mind and get serious about something for once in your life. Commit to actually study the Bible. Do not act like a Goober! The Bible is too important to be flippant. God's Word has too much to say for you to be nonchalant about it.

Big, scary words? You do not understand? Is the word *interpretation* too big and scary? Are Bible words too much to handle?

I do not think so. I do not think you are dumb.

I have never been one who dumbs down my message for teens, as if teens are somehow unable to grasp deep theology. You are intelligent when you want to be. The fact that you are reading this right now proves my point. You might be reading it because you feel like you are supposed to, but you are still reading it.

When you finally get real with God, you stop joking about the big, scary words and start working at knowing the mind of God. Start to work at interpreting Scripture.

Interpretation Defined

Interpretation is not a big, scary word. It is a simple word. It means "the meaning."

Whew! That was scary!

To find the interpretation of something means that we are finding the meaning of something.

When we are reading the Bible and we ask, "What does this mean?" we are actually asking, "What is the interpretation?"

When we learn the steps to interpret a biblical text, we are working to find the simple meaning of the text. We want to know what God says.

The title of this chapter is "INTERPRETATION – What is God Saying?" When we discover the interpretation (or meaning) of Scripture, we are discovering the mind of God.

Not Man's Interpretation

People might say, "Yeah, but *man* wrote the Bible. *Man* has errors. *Man* can mess up everything. *You* might say one thing, but *I* might say another. Who's right?"

Good question.

Is it up to us to *determine* the interpretation? No. We do not *determine* the interpretation. We *find* it. We *discover* it. We do our work and *search* for the interpretation.

True, man messes everything up. True, that man is full of error. But we are not following man; we are following God.

> **2 Peter 1:20-21** *Knowing this first, that no prophecy of the scripture is of any **private interpretation**. For the*

> *prophecy came not in old time by the will of man: but holy*
> *men of God spake as they were moved by the Holy Ghost.*

We are not allowed to choose what the Scripture says. We are called to obey what it says. We can only obey what we understand. We can only obey the Bible when we know the meaning.

Work at finding the interpretation of Scripture. It will not be easy, but it will be the way that God speaks to you.

One Interpretation. Many Applications.

Since the Bible is truth and is not open to private interpretation, it will be unchanging and unified. Nothing in the Bible contradicts itself. If I find a contradiction, I am wrong. The Bible is not wrong.

The Bible will never change meanings. The meaning (interpretation) of a text will always be the same, no matter who reads it or studies it.

If two different people read the same paragraph yet come up with two different interpretations, they are not both right. They cannot be. If one person's interpretation is "Jesus is God" and the other person's interpretation is "Satan is God," they are not both right. One of them is wrong.

Each text means only one thing. As we already discussed in the Introduction section, the Bible was written to be our guidebook. We are guided by principles. The principles that applied to the Old Testament Israelites are still valid today. The principles that Jesus taught his first century disciples are principles for 21st century disciples too.

Jesus meant one thing when he gave his parables. Paul meant one thing when he wrote his letters. Jude meant one thing. Peter meant one thing. Isaiah preached pointed sermons to God's people and each of those sermons only have one interpretation.

God has not changed. His Word has not changed. His *methods* have changed, but *He* has not changed.

Each Scripture you read has only one truth to it. If someone else claims another truth that is contradictory, one of you is wrong.

On the other hand, living by principles means that one truth can have many applications. The interpretation can be applied to life in several different areas.

The truth does not change, but how we live that truth does. One interpretation. Many applications.

For example, read 1 Corinthians 8:1-3:

> *1 Corinthians 8:1-3 Now as touching things offered unto idols, we know that we all have knowledge. Knowledge puffeth up, but charity edifieth. And if any man think that he knoweth any thing, he knoweth nothing yet as he ought to know. But if any man love God, the same is known of him.*

The interpretation can be simplified as: *"Knowledge is not the basis of Christian behavior. Love is."*

But the application is endless. The application of that principle spans time. *Love* is the principle for every Christian, not just for the Corinthians. The application of love might look different today than it did when Paul originally wrote this, but the principle remains intact. Love, to the Chinese person, is different from the love that a Romanian will show. Christian love during the Spanish

Inquisition would look different than Christian love today. Truth is applied differently in different cultures and eras, but the truth itself is always the same.

One Idea

Remember all that talk about one idea? The "Big Idea" stuff from Chapter Three is what interpretation is all about. When we work to discover the Big Idea, we work to discover the interpretation.

We are asking the question, "What is God saying?"

Finding out what God said in the past is how we understand what He is saying to us in the present.

An easy way to simplify what God said is to boil everything down to one summarizing Big Idea. Hence, BIBS—the Big Idea Bible Study.

The remainder of this book will be dedicated to discovering the Big Idea and working to whittle an entire text down to one summarizing statement. My professor, Pastor Jason Gaddis of Southwest Baptist Church in Oklahoma City, used to always ask, "Which is easier to catch—a rock, or a handful of sand? Should a friend toss you one tennis ball or a bucket full of tennis balls?"

Simpler is better.

Boiling the text down to one Big Idea is a tough task, but if we take it a step at a time, it will be simple. The Bible is full of ideas— rocks—and it is our job to discover them and apply them to our own lives.

Preparation

The BIBS format uses the analogy of a tree to picture the Big Idea. We are using several words and word pictures to describe the same thing. *Tree* is the same as *interpretation* or *meaning*. *Big Idea* is the summary of "what God is saying."

Interpreting Scripture is not easy, but it is simple. The next chapter will detail the first steps you will take in interpretation. After you choose an appropriate text, the steps you follow are:

- Read
- Reread
- Flag Words

Trunk and branches

In order to form our tree (Big Idea), we have to break it down to its individual parts—1) the trunk and 2) the branches.

Chapter 8 will deal with the trunk. In order to discover the interpretation of a text—or the tree—we must first start with the base—the trunk. The trunk answers the question, "What is God talking about?"

You will learn to discover the trunk by putting your text through these steps:

- Boil it down to a word
- Expand it to a phrase
- Summarize it in a sentence

Chapter 9 fills in the tree with all the branches and leaves. It completes the Big Idea. It is the bulk of the content, and it is discovered by these final steps in the BIBS process:

- Find the question word
- Restate it as a question
- Answer the question

The BIBS Process

The first step in the BIBS process is to **observe**. Gather information from the birds-eye perspective. Step back and look at background, language, culture, author, style, genre and as much behind the scenes stuff as you can.

Then, **interpret**. Follow the steps listed above. Find out what God is saying. Simply, the BIBS interpretation process is as follows:

- Read
- Reread
- Flag words
- Word
- Phrase
- Sentence
- Question
- Answer(s)
- Combine (Big Idea)

Finally, **apply**. The last stage of the BIBS process is to take what God *said* and translate it into what God is *saying*. If God is speaking, listen. When you listen to God, He shows you all kinds of things to fix.

Application makes the old, dry, boring and dusty Bible a living, exciting, new, fresh and life-changing Book. Part Three of this book is dedicated to applying what we interpret. It answers the question, "What is God saying *to me*?"

CHAPTER 7

FIRST STEPS

My Man-Child

I was a new dad. Beaming with pride, I held up my new man-child, Abraham Wyatt Rench, and looked him in the eye.

"Grow up and be tough, son." I said.

Then I put him in a headlock and started wrestling with him. I put him in a submission hold. I twisted him around and put him in an arm-bar.

He just cried.

Cry-baby. I couldn't wait until he grew up so I could *really* wrestle. To dads, babies are boring until they can wrestle. All the moms love the little babies. They stand around and coo at the babies. They hold the babies, snuggle the babies and kiss the babies. Abe would come home from church smelling like a woman's perfume. Uugh!

It was not until Abe was older that he finally got... fun! He would crawl around and we could finally wrestle. Abe was Dad's new favorite toy. A son is way better than an iPhone!

First Steps

Once Abe took those first steps I knew it would not be long until we would be having full on beat-downs with Dad, the uncles and the cousins. Abe is the second youngest of the six boy cousins, so before he was mobile he had to sit back and watch the older boys play. Now he is right there in the middle of them.

But it took a while to get there. They are called baby steps for a reason. Babies fall a lot.

The first steps that Abe took were super shaky. He was so nervous about falling, so he would always drop to a crawl instead of walk. Finally, gathering the nerve, he let go of our hands and took a couple steps.

YAY! We all cheered him on!

Then his big bobble-head made him top heavy and he plunked over like a domino. But he was victorious! Never again would his baby dreams and ambitions be suppressed! He was free!

His first steps were exciting. They were not perfect, but they were a start. They were simple and short. They did not get him very far, but they at least started him on his journey.

Your First Steps

When we talk about your first steps, we are talking about a couple things:

1) The first steps on your new journey of studying the Bible
2) The first steps (Steps 1-3) in the BIBS process.

If this is your first time getting serious about your Bible reading, your first steps will be shaky. You will fall down and have a rough time. Remember, you are going places! Nothing can hold you down! You're free! Start your Bible study journey, and do not look back. When (not *if,* but *when*) you fall down, get back up and keep on going. Baby steps turn into adult steps in time.

Sometimes the hardest part of Bible study is just getting started. You are not sure how to do it, you are anxious about the process, you do not have much time, or you are unclear of where it is going. You have likely started before but quit.

For me, the simpler any process is, the easier it is to start. That is why these first steps are so simple. Just start stepping. There might be hard times, but keep on stepping. Usually, if you can take the first steps, the rest will follow.

The hardest part is starting, so the first steps are designed to be really easy. Just... step.

Choose Your Text – "Step ½?"

Okay, so, technically this is a step, but I am not calling it *Step 1* because it is so easy. Maybe we can call it *Step ½*. It is like the floor mat you use to clean off your shoes right before you take Step 1.

Choosing your text is easy. Why? Because "All Scripture is given by inspiration of God, and is profitable..." (2 Timothy 3:16a) No matter where you turn in Scripture, you will be able to find something that is profitable.

It will not all be *equally* profitable, because your needs are not the same as your dad's needs, your teacher's needs or your friend's needs. Your needs are unique to you, so the profit in one passage might be more helpful to you than it is to someone else. But it is all profitable.

Anywhere you turn in the Bible will bring you some profit. You can be helped by every passage. Wherever you turn, apply the BIBS principles and you will find a way to be helped.

Even though you *can* be helped by any random text, that does not mean that you *should* be random in your Bible study. You should not just flip open your Bible anew each day and half-heartedly see what God reveals to you that day.

Rather, I would recommend a more systematic approach. Choose a book of the Bible to study, and get into the author's flow of thought. Study the Big Idea of the book by reading broadly (observation) each day, and also working on a deeper daily study of a smaller passage (interpretation).

There are a number of ways you can choose your text, but the following are a few suggestions:

Whole book. Study a whole book of the Bible. The book might be long or short, but it will have a Big Idea. Consider working on the overall theme of a book. Start on a small book at first, and work up from there. Perhaps the book of Philippians will be a blessing (here's a hint: it has a lot to say about joy).

Paragraph markings. Another way to choose a Bible text to study is to notice the paragraph markings in your Bible (looks like a backwards *P* or *D*). The paragraph divisions are not inspired (man divided the Bible into chapters, paragraphs and verses so we could read easier), but the paragraph divisions can serve as a guide to finding chunks of thought. New ideas often start with new paragraphs, and one Big Idea might emerge from a single paragraph section.

I have a Cambridge Cameo Bible that is sectioned off into paragraphs rather than verses. The poetry sections like Psalms, Proverbs and places in the prophets are laid out like modern poetry—each new phrase begins on a new line—and the rest of the Bible looks like a regular book—with big, flowing paragraphs rather than verse divisions. I love it! I read that Bible completely differently because I can get into the author's flow of thought. I read the story of David running from Saul like different scenes in a play. I read the dialogue between Job and his friends as if I am reading a novel. It makes the stories come alive, and I am able to think of the characters as real-live humans rather than mystical creatures from ancient history.

Section divisions. If you have a study Bible, your reading may already be sectioned off for you. Many study Bibles include headings that introduce each little unit of thought. Each heading breaks that chapter into smaller chunks of Scripture, like a Hershey's chocolate bar breaks into smaller chunks. Many times, choosing your text is as simple as choosing one of the chunks that someone else chose for you.

Devotional books. When we introduced the BIBS process to my youth group, we had an accompanying BIBS devotional book. The

BIBS devotional is designed to be both deep and wide. Each day, the teen would read several chapters to get into the flow of thought (wide), but he or she would also spend time interpreting a smaller section of Scripture already chosen for them (deep). Consider using the BIBS devotional, or use a devotional of your own. These devotionals will give you a text for the day's study.

In addition, certain reading plans section off your texts for you. Some reading plans have a daily reading devotion as well as a daily portion of Scripture to read along a topic. If these Scriptures are a help to you, consider using them as your text to interpret each day. No matter where you turn in Scripture, you will have God's truth.

Step 1: Read

Like I said, the first steps are the simplest. Do you think you can handle this one? Are you ready for it? Here goes...

Step one: read.

That's it. Just read it. After you choose your text (in Step ½), read it. Just read it. Your best tool will be reading. Try to get a broad idea of what it is saying.

Come on... you have been doing this since Kindergarten, right? Anyone can read. Unless you are listening to an audiobook version of this book right now, I know you can read. You are reading this BIBS book... now go read the Bible.

Reading is so simple. It is such an easy step. Just read.

Read the text. Try to get something from it. Read carefully and deliberately. Do not just breeze through it, but really read it as if it is a letter from a friend. Read it as if it matters—because it does.

Step 2: Reread

Step Two gets a little more complicated: **reread**. Not too bad, right?

After you finish reading the text the first time, go back and read it again. It is just a few verses. Think harder this time. Try to get an overall idea of what is going on in the story. Try to notice words that repeat.

Ignore the voice in your head that says, "I don't get this!" That dumb voice will show up every day if you let it.

Spend time rereading your text. Mull it over. Meditate on it. Think about it. Reread it 2 or 3 times, then 2 or 3 times more.

Start forming questions. Start thinking like the author. Why would he write this? What is he trying to get across?

Pull up your chair next to Paul as he is writing to Philemon, his old friend. Imagine Philemon as he is reading the letter from Paul. What is going on in Paul's head? What is Philemon thinking? How does Paul expect the reader to respond?

Read and reread with all the vigor and excitement you put into reading a novel. I was an avid reader of fiction in high school. I would get immersed into a book. I would live in the story. I would feel what the characters felt and I would think like the author wanted me to think. I was carried by the words on the page.

Let that happen with the Bible. Let the words live in you. Let the truth carry you. Let the emotion of the Psalms be real to you. Let the passion of the author speak to you. Read, reread and reread some more.

Step 3: Flag Words

As you read and reread your text, you will come across words you do not understand. **Flag key words** or repeating words. Notice unfamiliar phrases or references. Either mark them and come back to them later, or get your tools out and look them up as you go.

Remember your tools from Chapter 5? Refer to your cross-references, concordance, study Bible, dictionary, atlas or online Bible for further insight.

Sometimes, the key that unlocks the puzzle of the whole text is in a simple word definition. At other times, understanding a cultural reference or researching a strange phrase will clear up a confusing passage.

As you reread the text, notice the words that keep repeating themselves. Notice variations of the same word. Notice any restatement or definitions given in the text. Be alert to themes and be attentive to words that are unclear to you.

One benefit to working with online reference Bibles or computer software is the speed with which you can define words. One click reveals a pop-up window with the definition of any confusing word and a link to every verse that word is found in. What a computer can do in minutes requires much more time with a physical book.

The definitions of words are important. Do not ignore big words. Look them up.

A One-Question Pop Quiz

My father-in-law taught a biblical counseling class at a Bible college near his house. Each week he would give a quiz over the assigned reading. One week early in the semester, the chapter title was called "Nouthetic Counseling." The entire chapter talked about how to counsel from the Bible, how to be led by the Spirit, how to give hope in a counseling situation and how to give assignments that will bring lasting change to the counselee. The Bible college students walked into class having studied the ins and outs of the chapter. They knew the answers to all the questions the professor would ask.

When they received their quiz, they read one question: "Define *nouthetic*."

Almost everyone in the class failed. They had a general idea of what the word meant based on what the chapter was about, but no one had taken the time to look up the definition of the word.

Words are important. Do not ignore words.

Baby Steps

So far so good, right? The first steps are baby steps. They are simple, short and easy to do. You have all the tools that you need and you have all the brains that you need.

Do you want to hear from God? Do you want to know what He is saying?

If so, commit to knowing Him through His Word.

CHAPTER 8

THE "TRUNK"

I Can't See the Tree!

Have you ever heard the saying, "Can't see the forest for the trees?" It is an old saying that means you are losing sight of the big picture. It is as if you are standing with your nose stuck in the bark of a tree, saying, "There's no forest! It's a lie! I can't see any forest!"

You have lost sight of the big picture. You have forgotten what you are looking for.

I am going to rephrase the saying this way: "Can't see the tree for the leaves." Think of yourself way up in the limbs of the tree, straddling a thick branch with a microscope between your legs, focusing on one of the leaves. You are looking with one eye down the eyepiece of the microscope and saying, "There's no tree! It's a lie! I can't see a tree!"

No. You are so deep into the tree that you cannot see the big picture. It's a tree!

Find the Tree

Bible study is not entirely about depth. It does not take a microscope to see a tree. Some people go so deep into Scripture that they lose sight of reality. It seems like they lose their common sense.

Sometimes you need to set the microscope aside. Stand back and look at the whole tree.

In this Bible study, your job is to find the tree. Stand back and look at the text. Take in the whole picture. Form the Big Idea one step at a time.

The TRUNK - "What is God Talking About?"

In finding the tree, you are trying to answer the question, "What is God talking about?" What is this text about overall?

If the Big Idea is like a tree, then start with the main support—the trunk. Start broadly. The steps to study the text and find the trunk are as follows:

- Boil it down to a **word**
- Expand it to a **phrase**
- Summarize it in a **sentence**

Step 4: Word

You have read and reread.

You have looked up confusing words and noticed repeating words.

Now it is time to play a game. Think of it like a word-association game. Or, think of it as the game you would play as a kid, staring up at the shapes of the clouds and blurting the first word that would come to your mind.

Step 4 is as simple as this: **summarize the text in one word.** As you read and reread the text, what is the one word that keeps popping into your mind? What word keeps repeating itself? What word seems to sum everything up?

Is the text about God? Is it about love? Or grace? Or sin? Or repentance?

Grab a sheet of paper and write down several possibilities. The BIBS process will eliminate most of your list, but at first, write down all possibilities. Answer the question: "What is this text about?"

The word might be a major Bible topic, it might be a person or it might be an idea. It might be about a sin, a temptation, a blessing or a concept. It might be positive or it might be negative.

What is the text about? What word comes to mind?

EXAMPLE

Try Step 4 for yourself. First, read, reread and flag words in the following text:

> **Psalm 117** *O praise the Lord, all ye nations: praise him, all ye people. For his merciful kindness is great toward us: and the truth of the Lord endureth for ever. Praise ye the Lord.*

Having read, reread and flagged words in that Psalm, what is one word that might sum up the entire text? What word is repeated? What is this text about?

In one word, we can summarize this two-verse Psalm: *praise.*

What is this Psalm about? Praise. What word was repeated over and over? Praise.

The one-word summary is not exhaustive. This Psalm is not telling us everything about praise, nor does the one word even tell us whom to praise. The one-word summary is not a complete definition of the text. It is just a start.

Step 5: Phrase

In Step 4, the word is meant to be a first reaction. It might change, because it is so broad.

If your word is *praise,* as it was in our example, a ton of questions should come to mind. What about praise? What kind of praise? Where do we praise? Who are we to praise? Who is praising? Why should we praise? Is praise good or bad?

Not every question has answers, but your questions will help you take Step 5 in the BIBS process: **expand the word to a phrase**.

Read (Step 1) and reread (Step 2) the text. Look up words you do not know (Step 3). Study and think. Come up with a word that the text is about (Step 4), and then expound on that word (Step 5).

You will not have a full sentence yet; merely narrow the thought. If the word is *praise,* read the text and find out what the text is saying about praise. If it is *love,* perhaps the phrase will be *love God,* or *love others.* If the word is *sin,* the phrase might be *judgment of sin* or *the sin of mankind.*

When you expand the word to a phrase, you might only add a word or two. You will not have a complete subject and verb.

Do not get ahead of yourself in the process. Resist the urge to write a big, long sentence or explain *everything* in the text. Keep it simple. Someone once coined the acronym K.I.S.S.: Keep It Simple, Stupid! The simplest way to sum up a text is to start with a word and then expand it to a phrase.

In Psalm 117, the word was *praise* or *praising.* Expand that to a phrase and it becomes *praising the Lord.* Simple and easy.

Let's take it a step further...

Step 6: Sentence

We are moving from broad to narrow, like a funnel. We started with a word (broad) and are steadily limiting it (narrow). Now, more limiting than a phrase, here is Step 6: **expand the phrase to a sentence.**

A sentence is a complete thought. It has a subject and verb. It is a standalone concept.

If the question is "What is God saying?" then the sentence is the answer. "God is saying in this text that..." Whereas the word is expanded to a phrase, the phrase is expanded to a sentence.

At this point in the process, you are whittling down your list of words and phrases. This step will help you cull through the options and choose one or two.

The sentences can be long or short, but shorter is better. If your phrase has a subject, add a verb. If your phrase has a verb, add a subject or complement to make it a complete sentence.

Our example phrase from Psalm 113 was: *praising the Lord*. What about praising the Lord? Who should praise the Lord? Do not come up with the sentence on your own. Base it on the text.

> **Psalm 117** *O praise the Lord, all ye nations: praise him, all ye people. For his merciful kindness is great toward us: and the truth of the Lord endureth for ever. Praise ye the Lord.*

If you could boil this text down into a sentence, what is this text talking about? What is God saying?

Expanding the phrase to a sentence is simple: "We should praise the Lord." That is a full sentence—a complete thought. It is definite. It is concise. It is a rock (remember the Big Idea: it is easier to catch a rock than a handful of sand).

To move from phrase to sentence, all we had to do was add a subject and verb. Asking a question like, "Who should praise the Lord?" makes us reread the Psalm to find the answer. It is written to God's people—us—so *we* should praise the Lord. The opening and closing sentence to the Psalm is a command, so the sentence will be worded like a command: "We should praise the Lord."

Your sentence might be a command to obey, a truth to believe, or a sin to cease. It might be a doctrine to understand or a story of encouragement. It might be a pithy proverb or an in-depth dissertation. Any way you look at it, the sentence is the basic answer to a basic question: what is this text about—what is God saying?

Summary

In summary, the way to answer the question "What is God talking about?" is to follow this progression:

- Read
- Reread
- Flag Words
- Boil Down to a Word
- Expand to a Phrase
- Summarize in a Sentence

Once you can do that, you are well on your way to knowing God through His Word. Is the BIBS process the only way to know God? No. God can encourage you through one word or a single verse pulled from Scripture.

Sure, most people pull single verses out all the time. You see verses on walls as decorations, in frames and on billboards. There is no problem with that.

But a healthy diet of Scripture must be more than a verse here or there. Spiritual nourishment must be more than "candy, pop and ice cream."

Get into your Bible. Dig deep and read wide, and you will see what God *really* has to say to you as you get into His Word.

EXAMPLES

Try the following texts from various genres (gospels, epistle, parable, and narrative). After you observe and then read and reread the texts, what is the word that comes to mind? How would you expand them into phrases? What words would you add to make them sentences?

GOSPELS

> **Matthew 20:25-28** But Jesus called them unto him, and said, Ye know that the princes of the Gentiles exercise dominion over them, and they that are great exercise authority upon them. But it shall not be so among you: but whosoever will be great among you, let him be your minister; And whosoever will be chief among you, let him be your servant: Even as the Son of man came not to be ministered unto, but to minister, and to give his life a ransom for many.

WORD: _____

PHRASE: _____

SENTENCE: _____

_____

(See endnote for example answers.)[1]

EPISTLE

The book of Matthew (previous example) is one of the gospels and includes stories of Christ's life on earth. The gospels are not specifically written to one church like the epistles are. The next example is a letter to a baby church:

> **1 Thessalonians 1:6-8** *And ye became followers of us, and of the Lord, having received the word in much affliction, with joy of the Holy Ghost: So that ye were ensamples to all that believe in Macedonia and Achaia. For from you sounded out the word of the Lord not only in Macedonia and Achaia, but also in every place your faith to God-ward is spread abroad; so that we need not to speak any thing.*

WORD: _____

PHRASE: _____

SENTENCE: _____

_____

(See endnote for example answers.)[2]

PARABLE

A parable has been described as an earthly story with a heavenly meaning. The parable of the Good Samaritan is a familiar story to modern readers. A Jewish man is walking down the road where he is robbed and beaten, left for dead. Two religious Jews see him but pass by, not helping him. Finally, a Samaritan—the Jews' enemy— sees the man and helps him, going overboard to show love to this stranger. With that in mind, consider this text:

*Luke 10:25-37 And, behold, a certain lawyer stood up, and tempted him, saying, Master, what shall I do to inherit eternal life?— He said unto him, What is written in the law? how readest thou? And he answering said, Thou shalt love the Lord thy God with all thy heart, and with all thy soul, and with all thy strength, and with all thy mind; and thy neighbour as thyself. And he said unto him, Thou hast answered right: this do, and thou shalt live. But he, willing to justify himself, said unto Jesus, And **who is my neighbour?** And Jesus answering said, A certain man went down from Jerusalem to Jericho, and fell among thieves... [parable of the Good Samaritan told here] ... Which now of these three, thinkest thou, was **neighbour unto him** that fell among the thieves? And he said, He that shewed mercy on him. Then said Jesus unto him, Go, and **do thou likewise**. (emphasis added)*

WORD: _____

PHRASE: _____

SENTENCE: _____

_____

(See endnote for example answers.)[3]

NARRATIVE

The book of Daniel includes many familiar stories (Shadrach, Meshach, Abednego thrown in the fire; Daniel in the lion's den; Nebuchadnezzar turned into an animal) as well as some detailed prophecy. Truths emerge from narrative stories, and you need to read the whole context (the whole chapter or more) to see the point that is being made. (For more information on interpreting narrative, see Appendix 1.) Consider this verse:

> **Daniel 1:8** *But Daniel purposed in his heart that he would not defile himself with the portion of the king's meat, nor with the wine which he drank: therefore he requested of the prince of the eunuchs that he might not defile himself.*

Look up verses 1-7 to see what Daniel was going through in his life (observation). Once you have read, reread and flagged words, write your answers here:

WORD: _____

PHRASE: _____

SENTENCE: _____

_____

(See endnote for example answers.)[4]

_____

[1] Matthew 20:25-28
WORD: The word that repeats itself is *minister* or *servant*. In the observation stage you would have read the whole story: a mom wants her two sons to be great. In our text, Jesus is making a point to reply to her.
PHRASE: Several phrases are possible: *being a servant; Jesus as a servant; lowly servant; ministering to others; a servant's greatness.*
SENTENCE: Greatness is in serving others.
[2] 1 Thessalonians 1:6-8
WORD: Some key words might be *followers, ensamples (examples),* or *sounded.* The point is that this baby church is having an impact on the world through their godly lives. People could look at them and see that Christ had changed them for the better. I will choose the word *example.*
PHRASE: What are they examples in? Or to whom are they being examples? The phrase might be *examples in their faith, godly examples,* or *examples to others.*
SENTENCE: The Thessalonians had an exemplary faith.
[3] Luke 10:25-37
WORD: The word can be *neighbor, love* or *mercy*; perhaps *Christianity.*
PHRASE: Since the text is taken as a whole, the phrase considers the words before and after the parable. The phrase could be the following: *loving others, real Christianity, being a neighbor to others, being neighborly,* or *love of strangers.*
SENTENCE: We need to have real Christianity. Or: We should show love to others.

4 Daniel 1:8 (or 1:1-8)

WORD: In flagging words, you found definitions to key words like *purposed* and *not defile*. Sometimes your word might actually be two words (i.e. not defiled).

PHRASE: The phrase could be *Daniel's purpose, Daniel purposed in his heart, not being defiled,* or *keeping from sin.* Each of these phrases can be expanded on later.

SENTENCE: Daniel purposed to not defile himself. Or: Daniel purposed to live by faith.

CHAPTER 9

THE "BRANCHES"

Not Just a Trunk

A tree is not just a trunk. A tree without branches is called a fencepost or a telephone pole. Or dead.

A healthy tree has branches. The whole tree is made up of the trunk and branches. You cannot have one without the other.

If the trunk answers the question, "What is God talking about," the branches answer this question: "What is God *saying about* what He is talking about?"

The trunk would be barren and boring without the branches. The branches add bulk and beauty to the tree. The branches fill out the tree and carry the smaller details of the tree.

In Bible study, stopping at the trunk would be a shame. In your study, you will discover rich details and deep truths that will not exactly fit into your trunk. So what is their purpose?

Beauty in the Details

The purpose of all the details of the text is to act as branches to the tree. The details add bulk and beauty. They keep the text from being a barren and boring truth.

God could have chosen to convey His truth in a series of commandments and principles. At times He did just that (think of the 10 commandments). But imagine if the whole Bible were a series of one-line commandments. Phew! That would get boring. That would be like a forest of tree trunks—not very glorious.

Beauty comes through details and emotion. The Psalms would be horrible if they were missing details. The emotion of David's songs would be lost if he were to boil the Psalms down only to a trunk. Instead of the 23rd Psalm, we would read a simple commandment: Thou shalt trust the God who cares for you. It is not so beautiful when it is put that way.

The beauty of Psalm 23 is in the imagery and emotion. The Shepherd's care warms the heart. His protection calms all fears and His guidance gives courage. His provision is overwhelming, and His goodness gives hope.

> ***Psalm 23*** *The Lord is my shepherd; I shall not want. He maketh me to lie down in green pastures: he leadeth me beside the still waters. He restoreth my soul: he leadeth me in the paths of righteousness for his name's sake. Yea,*

though I walk through the valley of the shadow of death, I will fear no evil: for thou art with me; thy rod and thy staff they comfort me. Thou preparest a table before me in the presence of mine enemies: thou anointest my head with oil; my cup runneth over. Surely goodness and mercy shall follow me all the days of my life: and I will dwell in the house of the Lord for ever.

The truth may be simple—perhaps as simple as the trunk "The Lord cares for you"—but the branches are where the beauty and bulk come from. The branches are the offshoots. They are the supporting ideas. They are the truths shaped by beautiful word pictures. Rather than plain black and white, God's nature and nurture is portrayed through pictures of sheep, meadows, storms, feasts and rest.

Every text will have main ideas and supporting ideas. This chapter is about figuring out how to summarize the supporting ideas—the branches.

If the trunk asks the question, "What is God talking about?" then the branches ask the question, "What is God *saying about* what He is talking about?"

The trunk is general—word, phrase, sentence. The branches are specific.

The sentence (trunk) talks about the text. The supporting materials (branches) talk about the sentence.

Confused?

Don't worry. It is still a simple process.

As before, we want to put the text through a simple process. Small step by small step. Little by little. To find the branches, the steps in this chapter are as follows:

- Turn the sentence into a **question**
- Find the **answer**(s)
- **Combine** the trunk and branches (full tree)

If the Big Idea is a tree and we have already found the trunk, let us fill in all the branches—all the little details that describe or enhance the trunk.

Here's how...

Step 7: Question word

If you could turn your sentence into a question, what **question word** would you use? Is this a **who, what, where, when, why** or **how** text?

The first step to adding branches to the trunk is to turn the sentence into a question. Figure out what type of question is being asked.

- **Who?** Is this a text about someone? Is it directed to Christians? Non-Christians? Pastors? Demons? Is this a *who* text? *Example: Who should praise the Lord?*
- **What?** Is the text giving examples or things to know? Is it about something in particular? *Example: What does a praising person do?*
- **When?** Is the text giving specific times or instances? Is it teaching about a season or a timeline? Is it prophecy? Is it

history? Is it time-sensitive? Is it related to circumstances? *Example: When should a person praise God?*

- **Where?** Is the text about a place? Is it a location-specific truth? Is it a text about where to find certain truths? *Example: Where should a person praise the Lord?*
- **Why?** Does the text give reasons or examples? Does it answer the question *why? Example: Why should we praise the Lord?*
- **How?** Is the text explaining how to do something? Or how to think or act? Or is it perhaps a *how often* question? *How* questions can often be similar to *what* questions. *Example: How should we praise the Lord?*

You might think of other question words to use, but these are the main ones. Run your sentence (from Step 6) through these question words and figure out which one best fits the text.

Question

Once you have figured out which question word to use, rearrange the sentence into a question. Sometimes you will simply add the question word to the beginning of the sentence and reword it.

For example, our Step 6 sentence might be: "We should praise the Lord." If our question word is *why,* then our question now is: "**Why** should we praise the Lord?"

Restating the sentence in the form of a question forces you to find the answers. By figuring out what the text is about (the sentence, or trunk), we are able to take the next step and figure out what the text is *saying about* what it is about.

Confused again? That's okay.

Turning the sentence into a question leads automatically to the next step. Read on.

Step 8: Answer(s)

Once you have the basic question, simply **answer the question from the text.** Use as many answers as you might need. These answers will fill out your tree with all the leaves and branches.

If your question is broad enough, most details from the text will fit into an answer somehow. Obviously, if it is a tiny, minute detail, it might not fit directly to the trunk. That is okay.

What we are looking for at this stage is the Big Idea. While we have taken plenty of time to *narrow* our idea through our funnel (word, phrase, sentence, question, answers), we still are not so deep that we have lost sight of the big picture.

It is still a tree, after all. Do not approach it with a microscope. If you need to, stand back and look at the tree. Step back from the text. Yes, we are being more detailed than before, but not so much that we try to fit every detail into our answer.

Step 8 is not a science—you will not do exactly what the next person does. It is not mathematical—it does not have one set answer you can discover. The specific wording is subjective—it depends on how you look at the text. The *truth* is not subjective— there is only one correct interpretation—but how you word the truth might be different from how others word it.

Go to the text. Analyze your question. Find the biggest answers.

Sometimes, the answers are obvious, as in our previous example question: "Why should we praise the Lord?"

Psalm 117 O praise the Lord, all ye nations: praise him, all ye people. For his merciful kindness is great toward us: and the truth of the Lord endureth for ever. Praise ye the Lord.

Two clear answers to that question emerge. They are the two branches:

- Because his merciful kindness is great toward us.
- Because the truth of the Lord endures forever.

Once you know the question, the answers are easy. Form the question (Step 7), then look to the text for the answers (Step 8).

Step 9: Combine

The final step of interpretation is the easiest and the hardest.

It is the easiest step because you simply combine the question and answers into one sentence. It is the hardest step because you are working to boil *everything* down to one little, itty, bitty sentence. You will be frustrated, thinking, "There is SO much here... How in the world do I simplify this to *one sentence?!* I hate this BIBS book!"

Do not get mad. Do not throw your BIBS book across the room. Just stop and think.

Think about what the text is saying. Think about Chapter Three on the Big Idea. Ask yourself, "What is the Big Idea? Does my sentence basically sum it all up?"

In short texts, the summary is easy. The Big Idea of Psalm 117 is straightforward: *We should praise the Lord because His mercy is great toward us and His truth endures forever.* The full tree emerges as you combine the trunk and its branches.

Other texts are more difficult than our example text, but they are not impossible. Think in general terms. Instead of "God feeds me, clothes me, and protects me from my enemies," generalize it: "God cares for me." If the text lays out several specific actions you are supposed to do as a Christian, summarize them by saying "living right."

Summarize, generalize and simplify your wording to arrive at your Big Idea. In your own personal study you will be able to get deep into the specifics, but for the purpose of the BIBS process, keep it simple. Remember K.I.S.S.: Keep It Simple, Stupid!

Congratulations!

If you complete Step 9 and combine all your study into one simple sentence, congratulations! You did it! You have learned to hear from God. You have interpreted Scripture. See? Interpretation is not so bad after all.

You are now an official BIBS-er. All you have left to do is apply the truth. You have made it through two of the three crucial steps to hearing from God (Observe and Interpret). You are much closer to

God than probably 99% of the rest of the world because you are actively drawing nigh to Him.

> *James 4:6-9a But he giveth more grace. Wherefore he saith, God resisteth the proud, but giveth grace unto the humble. Submit yourselves therefore to God. Resist the devil, and he will flee from you. **Draw nigh to God, and he will draw nigh to you**.*

When you draw nigh to God, He promises to draw nigh to you. Draw closer to God through His Word every day.

In the next section, you will learn how to take the "old, dry, boring book" from ancient times to today's world. You will learn that every Scripture is relevant to your life if you look at it correctly.

PART THREE

APPLICATION

CHAPTER 10

APPLICATION - WHAT IS GOD SAYING TO ME?

The Most Important Section

Application is essential but dangerous. It is essential in that every Bible text has some kind of application to life. It has to, or else God wasted His and a lot of people's time writing and preserving it. (In case you are wondering, God did not waste His time.)

Application is essential, but it can be dangerous because it can be done wrong. Remember the chapter about observation? Incorrectly applying a text like "Judas went and hanged himself" can lead to some big-time neck burns!

Application must be done in order to take the Bible from the ancient world to today, but it must be done with the correct principles. Rather than pulling a verse out of context and making it mean something that God never intended, train yourself to put a little extra work into your study and figure out what God is really saying (interpretation). Then, obey the Bible.

Many people are really good at Part One and Part Two of this book. They can observe the Scripture. They know how to read, study, memorize, recite, and interpret the Bible. They can tell you every Bible story from beginning to end. They have been in church since they were born and they can rattle off Bible verses like they are lyrics to the most popular songs.

They might even love God. They might be sincere. They might read their Bibles and really know a lot about God.

But they do not obey God.

They know a lot about the Bible—the stories, the highlights, the memory verses—but they do not know how to bring that knowledge down to real life. They know about the lives of Paul, Peter, Matthew, Daniel and Jesus, but they have never had faith like Peter or suffered the persecutions of Paul. They have never prayed like Christ or had a testimony like Daniel.

They know what church is but they have never worshiped. They know what type of music is right but they have never meant a word they have sung. They know that God is omnipresent—everywhere all at the same time—but have never changed what they do in private.

They have heard about the Philistines, Egyptians, and Samaritans but they do not know how they make any difference in today's world. They know God wants them to be holy, but they do not block dirty shows on TV.

In short, most people know *about* God. They have heard a lot *about* Him, but they have never listened *to* Him.

Application makes the Bible real. Relevance is not just a buzzword in Christianity today, and it is not reserved for hip, cool preachers. Every text has relevance. Everywhere you turn in Scripture you will find a truth for you. If you think hard enough about it and know what God said, you will know what He is still saying today.

What Is God Saying To Me?

Parts One and Two of this book answered the question, "What is God saying?" We looked long and hard at how to hear God's voice.

Once you hear God's voice, realize that it is not just a voice of the past. It is also a voice in the present. It is not only that God *said* it in the past, but right now in the present He *is saying* it still.

If God is still saying what He said in the past, ask yourself, "What is God saying *to me?*" Every truth can help you in some way.

Step 10: Apply

There is only one *interpretation* to each passage—there is only one right answer to what God *said*—but, when it comes to application (what God is *saying* to me) there are several directions to take.

107

What applies to you may not be what applies to someone else, and vice versa.

In order to apply the text to your life, ask yourself, "Overall, what did I learn?"

God speaks in many different ways through His Word. In your Bible study, maybe He spoke to you from one word, one phrase or the Big Idea. God is always speaking through His Word, so how did He speak to you through this text? How does it apply to you? What did you learn from it? How has it helped you? How has it encouraged you? What did it challenge you to do?

Application is where the hard work begins. It is easy to learn stuff about God. It is easy to know that you are supposed to watch your mouth, guard your mind, be in church, give the gospel, care for others, obey your parents and more.

Bible truths are easy to know but difficult to live. Every day should be a serious time between you and God. First, pray and ask Him to reveal hidden sin. Next, ask Him to help you overcome it. Finally, ask Him if there is even anything small in your life that could be changed. He will reveal sins in your life, and it is your job to change them through His power. Application requires a clear-minded, openhearted soul searching time before God.

Self deception

> **James 1:22** *But be ye doers of the word and not hearers only, **deceiving your own selves**.*

According to James 1:22, the more you hear the Word and do nothing about it, the more self-deceived you become. That is scary... you do not even know *right now* if you are deceived (otherwise you would not be deceived!).

Does that concern you? No one likes to be deceived. No one wants to be tricked or lied to. No one likes the feeling of the others going behind their backs.

If you do not want to be deceived, then obey God. You are only sure about anything in life when you are hearing God's Word and obeying it.

Conversely, every time you hear and understand it, but do nothing to obey it, you are adding to your own self deception. It is partly your own fault when you find out that you are deceived. Be a doer of the Word and not just a hearer.

DO Something!

Determine to not only know stuff about the Bible but to actually do stuff with your knowledge. If the Big Idea you find is, "Paul's desire to see the Thessalonians walk worthy drove him to self sacrifice," (taken from 1 Thessalonians 2:1-12) you can respond a couple different ways:

"That's nice. Paul sacrificed for others. What a swell guy. Time for me to go to school!"

Or...

*"Wow. Paul was so passionate about helping others, he sacrificed a lot. How have I **sacrificed** lately? I really haven't. Maybe I should.*

"What can I sacrifice?! I'm nothing special. What do I have to give in self-sacrifice?

"Well, I guess I DO have a little **money**. *It's not much, but I know I need to sacrifice something, so I'm going to start giving to missions every week by faith.*

"I don't have much, but I DO have some spare **time**. *I waste a lot on video games. I doubt Paul did that. I need to spend my time better. I'm going to limit my video games to 1 hour and spend the rest of the time on my devotions (or exercise, or writing notes, or...)*

"I don't have much experience, but I CAN **work**. *I want to donate my youth and my energy to help out wherever I can. Not for payment but to simply serve. I'll call the church today to see where I can volunteer."*

Make a plan

Once you have decided to do something, write out your plan. **Be specific.**

So that I am not deceived, I plan to:

- Sacrifice by committing to $2/week.
- Time my video games and stop at one hour total. I'll spend the spare time doing my chores, reading _____ (name the book), writing encouraging notes to _____ (name the people), and exercising for ____ minutes per day.

- I'm going to call my youth pastor and set up a time to do yard work around the church. I'll also ask him this week at church if there's anything I can do throughout the week.

Specifically, what is one thing you can do this week that will be acting on what you have learned from God's Word?

Make a plan and write it down.

Conclude in prayer

God speaks and you respond by promising to act on His Word. Conclude your devotions in prayer and ask God's help and strength to keep your commitments. (Daniel 1:8)

Examples

Part Four of this book includes several example passages of Scripture that are put through the BIBS process and then applied. If you are curious about how to make application real, read Part Four for ideas.

We are guided by principles. The Bible is full of principles—Big Ideas—that we are to obey. The particulars of how those principles play out are different in each era and culture, but the Bible truth is always the same. Part Four is not intended to be a legalistic twisting of the Bible's principles. It is intended to offer clarity as we work to bridge the timespan from the ancient world to the modern world. Keep reading for more insight.

PART FOUR

CONCLUSION

CHAPTER 11

EXAMPLES

Sometimes It Helps

Sometimes it helps me to see an example of what the author is talking about. You can only read so much explanation before you say, "All right! Enough theory! Show me how this actually works!"

Some people like examples. If that is you, this chapter is for you.

Others say, "Yeah, I get it. No need to show me an example."

That is okay. You do not have to read this chapter. You can scan it and file it in your mind as reference material.

I have tried to compile examples from various genres and various lengths of texts. Each example goes into a different level of detail— some examples last several pages and others are only a couple paragraphs.

Use this chapter as a reference. Figure out what words were used and why. Notice how words are flagged, defined and used in the overall Big Idea. Notice how the interpretation flows directly into the application.

Keep in mind that the application is not about legalism. The Bible is not a rulebook. It is not a to-do list book. The applications listed here are examples. The applications are simple ideas of how the principle might affect our everyday lives. In these examples you will find things you agree and disagree with. So be it. The point is, if this chapter can be a help to you in figuring out how to study your Bible, mission accomplished. I am glad.

The following chapter is in two sections. The first section is the detailed look at all three parts: Observation, Interpretation, Application. The Interpretation step involves all nine steps (read, reread, etc.) and adds notes where needed. The Application section provides ideas on how the principle might be applied in a Christian's life.

Detailed Examples

Psalm 117

O praise the Lord, all ye nations: praise him, all ye people. For his merciful kindness is great toward us: and the truth of the Lord endureth for ever. Praise ye the Lord.

OBSERVATION

We know very little about the Psalm itself, but because it is a Psalm, we understand that it is probably to God or about God.

INTERPRETATION

- **Read and reread the text.** Done. Didn't take long.
- **Flag words.** I understand all the words, but looking up certain words adds depth to my understanding.
- V2 - Great - Prevail. Have strength. Mighty. Confirm, give strength.
- V2 - Endureth for ever. Everlasting. Eternal. Unending future.
- **Word.** Praise
- **Phrase.** Praise the Lord
- **Sentence.** We should praise the Lord.
- **Question Word.** Why?
- **Question.** Why should we praise the Lord?

- **Answers:** 1) His merciful kindness and 2) His truth endures.
- **Big Idea.** We should praise the Lord because His mercy is great toward us and His truth endures forever.

APPLICATION

First, God is merciful to me. Why does He choose to be merciful? Why does He have to be merciful? What is He merciful toward? Why would He be called merciful? If He's merciful, that must mean that He is holding back some kind of wrath or punishment.

I certainly deserve a lot of punishment for my sin. I know my own heart; my own lusts. I know what I'm like when no one is around. And... wow... God shows mercy to me every day. What an amazing God! He is so longsuffering with my sin, and He allows me the chance to repent and forsake my sin. God, thank you for showing mercy.

Second, His kindness. God not only does NOT give me punishment when I deserve it, but he DOES give me things that I do not deserve.

Thank you, God, for being so merciful to me. Thank you, on top of that, for being kind and giving me so much. I don't deserve my healthy body, but You are kind enough to give it to me. I have a great family, parents who love me, a loving church to attend, friends who want to help me, I live in America and I'm spoiled rotten with all the conveniences you give me. Thank you, God.

Third, You're not only merciful and kind, but those qualities are GREAT toward me! Why would you offer me mercy even once? And why in the world do You KEEP being merciful and kind even when you know my heart?! You have heaped on the blessings over and over, and I never really thank you properly for it.

The second "branch" was about your truth. I was allowed to read Your very words to me. I can know that there's something true in my life because Your Word has never been proven wrong. It is Truth. And it's still around. And no matter how many people have tried and will try to attack it, it still endures. It's forever! It's eternal. No other book is like that. Thank you, God, that I can know Your Truth!

All this, God... Your merciful kindness that is GREAT toward me... and Your wonderful Truth that you allow me to know and study. How can I keep silent about you?! You're SO good to me! And I too often fail You. Forgive me, God. But more than that, I PRAISE you! Praise God for being SO good to me! Thank you God! I want to serve You more and MORE every day!

MY PLAN: So that I am not deceived, I plan to attend church this Sunday morning and night and REALLY take part in the praise portion of our services. I'm going to sing loud, concentrate on the words, have a heart of gratitude and let is show on my face this Sunday. Hopefully everyone will be able to tell this praise is finally real with me.

Parable – Luke 10:25-37

A parable has been described as an earthly story with a heavenly meaning. The parable of the Good Samaritan is a familiar story to modern readers. A Jewish man is walking down the road where he is robbed and beaten, left for dead. Two religious Jews see him but pass by, not helping him. Finally, a Samaritan—the Jews' enemy—

sees the man and helps him, going overboard to show love to this stranger. With that in mind, consider this text:

> And, behold, a certain lawyer stood up, and tempted him, saying, Master, what shall I do to inherit eternal life?-- He said unto him, What is written in the law? how readest thou? And he answering said, Thou shalt love the Lord thy God with all thy heart, and with all thy soul, and with all thy strength, and with all thy mind; and thy neighbour as thyself. And he said unto him, Thou hast answered right: this do, and thou shalt live. But he, willing to justify himself, said unto Jesus, And **who is my neighbour?** And Jesus answering said, A certain man went down from Jerusalem to Jericho, and fell among thieves... [parable of the Good Samaritan told here] ... Which now of these three, thinkest thou, was **neighbour unto him** that fell among the thieves? And he said, He that shewed mercy on him. Then said Jesus unto him, Go, and **do thou likewise.** (emphasis added)

OBSERVATION

Who wrote it, what's going on, why was it written?

Luke wrote this whole book as a testimony to Christ's humanity. Jesus was both God and man.

What's the context (previous chapters)?

Christ is far enough into His ministry to have called and trained His disciples, and is now sending them out two by two. God's authority has been passed to these common men rather than the religious leaders.

What type of writing is it? (Narrative? Parable? Psalm? Letter?...)

This text is a story about Jesus talking to a man about what it means to be a Christian, and he uses a parable to answer a question the man had.

INTERPRETATION

Read, re-read, flag words and look up, get an overall idea. How does it start? How does it end? Key words? Summary words?

It starts with a lawyer (someone who studies the Old Testament [OT] law) trying to trick Jesus into messing up. It ends with the lawyer being speechless at Jesus' knowledge and challenge of not only know the law but do it.

- V25 – Lawyers know the OT law inside and out, and they hate Jesus. This one tried to trip Jesus up (tempt) and asked Him what he thought was a hard question: "...eternal life?"
- V26 – Jesus doesn't answer. Lets HIM answer himself.
- V27 – Lawyer knows the law. Quotes the OT.
- V28 – Jesus: "Right. Keep the entire law perfectly and you'll be saved." (That's true. If someone COULD love God with ALL their heart, soul, strength and mind, they'd never sin. Only Jesus did that.) That made the lawyer feel dumb.

- V29 – He had to justify his dumb question that he answered for himself. Next dumb question—thinking he can trick Jesus: "Who IS my neighbor?"
- V30 – Again... no answer from Jesus. Instead, story-time.
- 30-35 – story of the Good Samaritan. The Jews *hated* Samaritans, so this lawyer hated this story.
- V36 – Story's done... now Jesus asks a new question, "Which one was *being* the neighbor?"
- V37 – Lawyer couldn't even say the word *Samaritan*. Jesus sure shut HIM up! Go and BE a neighbor; don't worry about trying to be all religious without it being real.

You've read and re-read and come up with a LOT of different ideas... so now what?

What is God saying?

Well, He's saying we ought to know the law, love God with all our heart, soul, mind, strength, have a heart for people's needs, care for the wounded, not be racist, and not be a hypocrite.

WRONG!

All those details might be in the story, yes, but *at the core,* **what is God saying?** It's easier to catch a rock than it is a handful of sand. Paul's not throwing you sand... he's throwing a rock! So **what is God saying?**

Word(s), phrase, question word, question (subject), answer (complement), combine (CIT)

- **Word(s):** Christianity (Or Salvation, or Love)
- **Phrase:** Real Christianity
- **Question word:** What
- **Question (subject):** What is real Christianity?
- **Answer (Complement):** A true love for God that overflows into a love for others.
- **Combine into CIT (Central Idea of the Text) or Big Idea:** A true love for God will transform the way that you treat others.

This Lawyer thought he knew everything there was to know about the Bible... and he probably did. It is possible he had almost all of the available OT memorized, but he missed the heart of the message. Jesus simply asked him to repeat what he knew about the *essence* of who God is: one worthy of ALL our heart, soul, mind and strength.

When the lawyer realized what just came out of his own mouth – that no one can have eternal life without following THAT formula (that he could only received eternal life by putting his faith in Christ) – he was shocked. This guy, Jesus, made sense!

So he trips up a little, tries to justify himself, and attempts to trick Jesus again (This guy never learns!) "Who's my neighbor, then?"

Jesus basically says, "That's not the question. The good Samaritan shows us the *real* question about Christianity is... who are YOU being a good neighbor to? It's not the other way around."

APPLICATION

So what? We know now what God is saying, but who cares? That was 2000 years ago! It's not a history lesson... it's a life-changing text if you let it be one for you.

What is God saying? – Interpretation.

What is God saying <u>to you</u>? – Application

You can have ALL the right things to say on the outside, but the very basics of Christianity say

1. You're saved by totally loving God enough to place your faith in Christ.

2. That love ought to overflow to everyone you know... friends, family, acquaintances, and even enemies.

Your love for God should transform the way your treat others.

Does it?

Or is there someone you hate? Anyone? Even someone who's done you VERY wrong?

How about your heart for others? How much love are you showing to the people that annoy you most?

If you're ever unkind to someone, whether intentionally or not, you're not being Christ-like. If you say you know God and you're a Christian, Jesus is saying there ought to be a spirit in you that only desires to fall more and more in love with God. Once you have that spirit, if it's real, you can't help but love everyone around you.

How patient are you with others?

How compassionate are you?

How much do you care about people's souls?

How much would YOU sacrifice for someone?

When was the last time you did something nice for someone who annoyed you?

By what you do for others, would people say you're a Christian?

Psalm 113

Praise ye the Lord. Praise, O ye servants of the Lord, praise the name of the Lord. Blessed be the name of the Lord from this time forth and for evermore. From the rising of the sun unto the going down of the same the Lord's name is to be praised. The Lord is high above all nations, and his glory above the heavens. Who is like unto the Lord our God, who dwelleth on high, Who humbleth himself to behold the things that are in heaven, and in the earth! He raiseth up the poor out of the dust, and lifteth the needy out of the dunghill; That he may set him with princes, even with the princes of his people. He maketh the barren woman to keep house, and to be a joyful mother of children. Praise ye the Lord.

OBSERVATION

Who wrote it, what's going on, why was it written? What's the context (previous chapters)? What type of writing is it? (Narrative? Parable? Psalm? Letter?...)

Perhaps written as a post-exilic thanks-Psalm to God, Psalm 113 is a song of praise to God, emphasizing his almighty goodness. This psalm was used in conjunction with the 114th – 118th psalms as a Hallel, or Hymn. These Psalms were usually the ones sung at particular festivals, possibly the feast of Tabernacles and the Passover.

Some would divide this passage into three sets of three verses each, and name the first set as the call to praise, the second as the substance of praise for who God is, and the third as the substance of praise for what God does.

INTERPRETATION

Read, re-read, flag words and look up, get an overall idea. How does it start? How does it end? Key words? Summary words?

Text:

1 ¶ Praise ye the LORD. Praise, O ye servants of the LORD, praise the name of the LORD.

This is the opening sentence of the call to praise. The psalm was sung to God, but it was directed at the people who were to do the praising.

2 Blessed be the name of the LORD from this time forth and for evermore.

The name of the Lord is brought into focus here. In majestic terms the Psalter calls the people to bless the Lord through all time. Whatever the time period is (pre-exilic, post-exilic, or other), the people of Israel have so much to thank God for.

3 From the rising of the sun unto the going down of the same the LORD'S name is to be praised.

Whether the implication is that praise should be given from horizon to horizon, or that praise should be given from dawn till dusk, the point is that unending praise should be rendered to the One who deserves it most.

4 The LORD is high above all nations, and his glory above the heavens.

This new section, or strophe, begins with the high and lofty view of God. There He is... high above all nations. His glory is above the heavens! Always looking up, the author tries to convey in words the glimpse of God's glory that he caught while thinking these thoughts.

5 Who is like unto the LORD our God, who dwelleth on high,

The author uses yet another stylistic approach and asks almost a foolish question—were it really a question seeking an answer. Who is like him? There is none like him.

6 Who humbleth himself to behold the things that are in heaven, and in the earth!

Humbleth

- 08213 shaphel shaw-fale'
- a primitive root; TWOT-2445; v

- AV- low 10, down 8, humble 7, abase 2, debase 1, put lower 1; 29
- to be or become low, sink, be humbled, be abased
- 1a) (Qal) to be or become low
- 1b) (Hiphil)
- 1b1) to lay or bring low, humiliate
- 1b2) to set in a lower place, show abasement
- 1b3) to make low, sit down[12]

Strong's and BDB both agree on the definition of this word directly from the Hebrew, and Webster adds the English definition as such: Made low; abased; rendered meek and submissive; penitent.[3]

What a thought! That God would have a Psalter describe him in such a way—almost with the idea of being brought low or even *penitent!* Just to look on his creation?! And he loves us? How can we do anything *but* praise him? This is drive. Motivation to praise him.

7 He raiseth up the poor out of the dust, and lifteth the needy out of the dunghill;

Here, it seems very probable that the author is using a quote or at least a reference to the song of praise that Hannah prayed after receiving a child in 1 Samuel 2. The words are almost verbatim.

---

[1] Strong's Concordance of the Whole Bible; Online Bible 2.00.04; #05800; OnlineBible.net

[2] Brown-Driver-Briggs' Hebrew Definitions; e-sword vs. 7.7.7; 2005; e-sword.net

[3] Webster's 1828 Dictionary of the English Language; e-sword vs. 7.7.7; 2005; e-sword.net

Dung-hill

- To sit on a, was a sign of the deepest dejection #1Sa 2:8 Ps 113:7 #La 4:5[4]
- 0830 'ashpoth ash-pohth' or 'ashpowth ash-pohth' or (contraction) shephoth shef-ohth'
- plural of a noun of the same form as 0827, from 08192 (in the sense of scraping); TWOT-2441b; n m
- AV-dung 4, dunghill 3; 7
- ash heap, refuse heap, dung-hill[5]
- Dung Heap, or place of refuse. To sit on a dunghill is significant of the lowest and most wretched condition. To turn a house into a dunghill, or be flung upon a dunghill, marks the extreme of ignominy.[6]

From absolutely the lowest possible condition of mankind, we go on to the next verse. The picture here is that there is no hope outside of God. Man is totally destitute in himself.

8 That he may set him with princes, even with the princes of his people.

Princes

- 05081 nadiyb naw-deeb'
- from 05068; TWOT-1299b
- AV-prince 15, nobles 4, willing 3, free 2, liberal 2, liberal things 2; 28
- adj

---

4 Easton's Revised Bible Dictionary; Online Bible 2.00.04; OnlineBible.net
5 Strong's Concordance of the Whole Bible; Online Bible 2.00.04; #05800; OnlineBible.net
6 International Standard Bible Encyclopedia; ISBE; e-sword vs. 7.7.7; 2005; e-sword.net

- inclined, willing, noble, generous
- 1a) incited, inclined, willing
- 1b) noble, princely (in rank)
- 1c) noble (in mind and character)
- noble one[78]

This word occurs quite frequently in our English Bible, mostly in the Old Testament. While it is never used to denote royal parentage, it often indicates actual royal or ruling power, together with royal dignity and authority. As a rule, the name is given to human beings; in a few instances it is applied to God and Christ, the angels and the devil.[9]

This exalted position is only what God can bring a person to. By saying that, I am not emphasizing the position attained but the one who is doing the raising—God himself. From the degradation in the previous verse to the high and lofty position of rulers and princes, one cannot but think of God's glory when he does all that for his people. The contrast is the shocking part of this passage in that the picture that is painted of man's degradation is so bleak, and the hope that is offered because of the life that is offered in God is like sunlight and fresh air to one who has been locked in a dank cave his whole life.

9 He maketh the barren woman to keep house, and to be a joyful mother of children. Praise ye the LORD.

If the previous verses refer to the song of Hannah, I cannot but conclude that here we have a reference back to Hannah's

---

7 Strong's Concordance of the Whole Bible; Online Bible 2.00.04; #5081; OnlineBible.net

8 Brown-Driver-Briggs' Hebrew Definitions; e-sword vs. 7.7.7; 2005; e-sword.net

9 International Standard Bible Encyclopedia; ISBE; e-sword vs. 7.7.7; 2005; e-sword.net

predicament and solution. God is the giver of grace through all ages, and it would do his people good to recognize and honor him because of it.

You've read and re-read and come up with a LOT of different ideas... so now what?

What is God saying?

Word(s), phrase, question word, question (subject), answer (complement), combine (CIT)

- **Word(s):** Praise
- **Phrase:** God deserves our praise
- **Question word:** Why
- **Question (subject):** Why does God deserve our praise?
- **Answer (Complement):** Because of who God is, how high he is, and how low we are. The contrast in view ought to help us see the reality of what God did and does for us.
- **Combine into Big Idea:** I cannot better phrase the words of the Jamieson-Fausset-Brown Commentary when they said: **God's majesty contrasted with His condescension and gracious dealings towards the humble furnish matter and a call for praise.**
- Or: Think on God and praise his name.

APPLICATION

So what? We know now what God is saying, but who cares? That was 2000 years ago! It's not a history lesson... it's a life-changing text if you let it be one for you.

What is God saying? – Interpretation.

What is God saying <u>to you</u>? – Application

Prayer – "Hallowed be thy name..." Revered, honored, lifted up. Begin your prayer recognizing your own position before God.

God, do I approach prayer as if you really are high and lifted up? Forgive my flippant attitude. Help me see you for who you are.

I want to start every day with a time of prayer, recognizing that God is high and holy. I want to be dependent on God. I want to praise and worship Him. In my daily prayer time, before asking for anything *from* God, I want to be sure to recognize who He is and all that He has done for me.

True Worship – I am low, God is high... Praise Him!

Reasons for reverence, worship, praise. God is high and holy. He is separate. When I worship Him—personally on my own and corporately at church—I want to focus on Him. I want His attributes to be on my mind. Rather than think of worship as a certain type of music, I want my worship to be sincere and real. I want to worship God by thinking about his holiness, by lowering myself in humility, and by recognizing His power over every part of my life.

In worshiping God, I want to sing deep, rich truths about Him. I want my thoughts and emotions to be driven by truth, not hype. I want to respond to God's goodness to me with true praise. I want to be careful to not lift myself up in praising Him, but I want to be sincere in recognizing all God's blessings in my life.

He has been so good to me. Praise His name.

Philippians 4:1-9

Therefore, my brethren dearly beloved and longed for, my joy and crown, so stand fast in the Lord, my dearly beloved. I beseech Euodias, and beseech Syntyche, that they be of the same mind in the Lord. And I intreat thee also, true yokefellow, help those women which laboured with me in the gospel, with Clement also, and with other my fellowlabourers, whose names are in the book of life. Rejoice in the Lord alway: and again I say, Rejoice. Let your moderation be known unto all men. The Lord is at hand. Be careful for nothing; but in every thing by prayer and supplication with thanksgiving let your requests be made known unto God. And the peace of God, which passeth all understanding, shall keep your hearts and minds through Christ Jesus. Finally, brethren, whatsoever things are true, whatsoever things are honest, whatsoever things are just, whatsoever things are pure, whatsoever things are lovely, whatsoever things are of good report; if there be any virtue, and if there be any praise, think on these things. Those things, which ye have both learned, and received, and heard, and seen in me, do: and the God of peace shall be with you.

OBSERVATION

Who wrote it, what's going on, why was it written?

Paul wrote Philippians to the church at Philippi when he was in prison.

Apparently Paul's just writing to encourage them. They aren't a bad church with tons of problems.

What's the context (previous chapters)?

Paul talks about the joy of real Christianity... of doing what God says to do! All over he's talking about living for Christ, rejoicing in his work, and being content in Christ alone.

What type of writing is it? (Narrative? Parable? Psalm? Letter?...)

It's a letter, so his big thoughts are probably not in a whole chapter like a story (narrative) would be, but in a few verses at a time.

INTERPRETATION

Read, re-read, flag words and look up, get an overall idea. How does it start? How does it end? Key words? Summary words?

- V1 – Stand fast in the Lord.
- V2 – Don't fight.
- V3 – Help them not fight! They're good ladies!
- V4 – Rejoice. Oh yeah... REJOICE!
- V5 – Have a testimony of gentleness. Let's take a break to remember: The LORD is at hand!
- V6 – Okay... back to standing fast... Don't worry. Combat *worry* with *prayer* with *thanksgiving*.
- V7 – Let God's *peace* keep you... not *worry*! God's peace is beyond anything you can comprehend.
- V8 – Finally (as in: the last thing in this list of how to stand fast), stand fast by thinking on *these things* (listed).

- V9 – And everything you've learned, received, heard and seen in me... DO it. Don't just KNOW it!
- When you do, God (you know, that amazing God of incomprehensible and mind-blowing peace) will be with you.

[Note: that's just a quick read-through! I just re-wrote exactly what the Bible said, right?]

You've read and re-read and come up with a LOT of different ideas... so now what?

What is God saying?

He's saying stand fast, don't fight, help people, rejoice, be gentle, pray, don't worry, be thankful, think right, follow godly examples, do what God says, and allow God's peace to rule in your heart.

WRONG!

He said all those things, yes, but *at the core,* **what is God saying?** It's easier to catch a rock than it is a handful of sand. Paul's not throwing you sand... he's throwing a rock! So **what is God saying?**

Word(s), phrase, question word, question (subject), answer (complement), combine (CIT)

- **Word(s):** Stand fast
- **Phrase:** I need to stand fast in the Lord
- **Question word:** How?
- **Question (subject):** How should we stand fast in the Lord?

[Note: You might be tempted to say "*Why* should we stand..." and think the answer (complement) is, "So we can have peace," but that's not the push of the text. Peace is a byproduct... one more wonderful blessing of God!]

- **Answer (Complement):** By not only *knowing* what God says but *acting* on it.

  [Note: I combined all the random ideas into *one overall idea:* doing what God says, or, acting on what God says.]

- **Combine into Big Idea:** Christians have to stand fast by not only *knowing* about God but actually *acting* on His truth.

APPLICATION

So what? We know now what God is saying, but who cares? That was 2000 years ago! It's not a history lesson... it's a life-changing text if you let it be one for you.

What is God saying? – Interpretation.

What is God saying <u>to you</u>? – Application

I need to stand fast. I need to stand fast by praying with thanksgiving. I need to stand fast by making sure I'm thinking on right things. I need to stand fast by acting on what I know is right.

[note: Application goes deep. Application goes as far as you want it. Too many times, people *start* with application ("I want to preach/teach this idea... I need to find a text that will back that up") but you *should* start with the text and see what GOD says first. THEN take it to application.]

136

Once I know what God says (I need to stand fast by acting on what He says to do), then I can *apply* it LOTS of different ways, and as narrow as you want.

Music. *If God commands me to stand fast in the Lord, and He says that one of the ways to do that is to think right... how can I fill my head with things that are godly (true, honest, just, pure, lovely, good report)?*

[Note: I COULD apply this with my speech, what I watch on TV, who I hang out with, what kind of cussing I put up with all day, where I'm going to college, what church I go to, what I read, etc.; but we're just focusing on one: music.]

Music paints pictures. So what kind of pictures am I allowing my music to paint in my head?

- Godly? (Philippians 4:8-9)
- Or worldly? (sensual, depressing, angry, loud, hateful, sad, unbiblical...)

SHORT EXAMPLES

Matthew 20:25-28

But Jesus called them unto him, and said, Ye know that the princes of the Gentiles exercise dominion over them, and they that are great exercise authority upon them. But it shall not be so among you: but whosoever will be great among you, let him be your minister; And whosoever will be chief among you, let him be your servant: Even as the Son of man came not to be ministered unto, but to minister, and to give his life a ransom for many.

- WORD: Minister or servant.
- PHRASE: A servant's greatness
- SENTENCE: Greatness is in serving others.
- QUESTION: How can we be great?
- ANSWER(S): Contrary to power and authority, greatness is in 1) humility and 2) service.
- BIG IDEA: Jesus' example shows us that only humble service brings greatness.

APPLICATION: I need to humbly serve. Not to be noticed, but to simply show love to others.

In church, at home, at school, with my friends, and with my enemies.

Humility – am I consumed with power and authority? Do I constantly worry about what others think of me? Or am I humble? Would I be willing to minister to others without expecting anything in return?

Service – do I enjoy serving others? Am I a servant? When was the last time I gave of myself? When was the last time I worked without expecting a paycheck or a free snack or time off? How selfish is my service?

Greatness – according to Jesus, am I on the track to greatness? I thought greatness was in being the loudest, most powerful one of my peers. Or having the greatest career and most money. If greatness is in humble service, how great am I becoming?

Daniel 1:8 (or 1:1-8)

But Daniel purposed in his heart that he would not defile himself with the portion of the king's meat, nor with the wine which he drank: therefore he requested of the prince of the eunuchs that he might not defile himself.

- WORD: Purpose
- PHRASE: Daniel's purpose
- SENTENCE: Daniel purposed to not defile himself.
- QUESTION: How did Daniel not defile himself?
- ANSWER(S): By purposing in his heart. By living by faith in God.
- BIG IDEA: Although he never knew the outcome, Daniel's clear purpose to live by faith led him to actions of faith.

APPLICATION: As a teen, Daniel was able to stand by faith in the face of the world ruler. He never compromised his morals even when his peers were against him, his education was anti-God and his accountability was gone. How? He had already purposed to not defile himself. He had made a pact with God. He purposed—"set hands violently on"—ahead of time, before the temptation occurred. He made up his mind prior to the temptation.

Am I that set (like, set in concrete) on my stand for God? What do I need to purpose to do? When the temptation comes, how will I be able to overcome it? I need to purpose to _____ (you fill in the blanks).

1 Thessalonians (Several Examples)

Open your Bible and see for yourself how to arrive at these Big Ideas. Would you agree or disagree? What are some specific applications that would help you?

1:6-8

And ye became followers of us, and of the Lord, having received the word in much affliction, with joy of the Holy Ghost: So that ye were ensamples to all that believe in Macedonia and Achaia. For from you sounded out the word of the Lord not only in Macedonia and Achaia, but also in every place your faith to God- ward is spread abroad; so that we need not to speak any thing.

- WORD: Examples
- PHRASE: Examples in their faith
- SENTENCE: The Thessalonians were examples in their faith.
- QUESTION: How were the Thessalonians examples in their faith?

- ANSWER(S): They received the Word, and it changed them.
- BIG IDEA: Because the Thessalonians let God's Word change them, their church's testimony spread worldwide!

APPLICATION: How am I letting the Word of God change me? I'm worried about being a Christian and being laughed at. They were bold. How'd they get so bold? The Word of God changed them.

How have I been changed recently? I can't change myself. I need God to change me. I need to get into God's Word. Before I can change the world, I need to change myself. I need to allow God to mold me into His image.

2:1-13

- WORD: Sacrifice
- PHRASE: Paul's self sacrifice
- QUESTION: Why did Paul sacrifice so much?
- ANSWER: He wanted to do everything he could to see the Thessalonians walk worthy.
- BIG IDEA: Paul's desire for the Thessalonians to walk worthy drove him to self sacrifice.

Application: _____

_____

_____

(See Chapter 10 for specific applications.)

2:13-20

- WORD: Persecution
- PHRASE: Standing Firm in Persecution
- QUESTION: Why does Paul want to see them stand firm in persecution?
- ANSWER(S): It brings glory and joy
- BIG IDEA: Paul commends the Thessalonians for standing firm in the face of persecution.

Application: _____

_____

_____

3:1-10

- WORD: Faith
- PHRASE: The Thessalonians' faith
- SENTENCE: Paul desires the Thessalonians' faith to mature.
- QUESTION: Why does Paul desire the Thessalonians' faith to mature?
- ANSWER: So that (v13) they will be unblameable on judgment.
- BIG IDEA: Paul desires the maturity of the Thessalonians' faith so that they will be unblameable on judgment.

Application: _____

_____

_____

On the following texts, try filling in the missing parts on your own. Work through the BIBS process and apply it to yourself.

4:1-12

BIG IDEA: A mature faith will grow in sanctification

- Moral (1-7)
- Love (v9)
- Work. Be honest. (11-12)

Application: _____

_____

_____

4:13-18

Doctrine of the Rapture. For this text, follow the BIBS process and try to arrive at the Big Idea on your own.

Application: _____

_____

_____

5:1-11

BIG IDEA: In light of Christ's return, we are to comfort and edify each other to good works.

Application: _____

_____

_____

5:12-22

BIG IDEA: With Christ's imminent return, the authentic church will teach right doctrine and pursue right living.

Application: _____

_____

_____

1 Thessalonians

The whole book of 1 Thessalonians has a flow of thought to it. As we discussed in earlier chapters about the Bid Idea, not only does a small text (a few verses) have a Big Idea, but whole chapters and books have Big Ideas too. Consider the following for the book of 1 Thessalonians:

You HAVE to be REAL.

All chapters:

- Ch. 1 – your life screams that you're real.
- Ch. 2 – I'll sacrifice for you because you're real. You're real because you can stand the real tests.
- Ch. 3 – Your faith is real because it deepens.
- Ch. 4 – Your faith is real because it shows.

- Chapters 1-4 Paul says, "Praise God, saints! Everything about you is REAL! You're an AUTHENTIC CHURCH!"

BOOK'S BIG IDEA: Authentic Faith

- AUTHENTIC faith shows. (Ch. 4)
- AUTHENTIC faith grows. (Ch. 3)
- AUTHENTIC faith endures. (Ch. 2)
- AUTHENTIC faith spreads. (Ch. 1)

APPLICATION: Is your faith authentic?

CHAPTER 12

USING BIBS

Daily BIBS Devotional

You can use BIBS several different ways. First, as a devotional method. My wife graduated from Bible college with a teaching degree, but, because of her major, took very few Bible study courses. She received general Bible overview classes but was never able to take the classes that taught her how to interpret Scripture. Shortly after we were married, she asked me if I knew of any good devotional books she could go through. I did not. Most of the devotionals that I had seen were shallow, pathetic things. They were either weak on Bible or they left you coming to your own conclusions. I wanted neither option.

I wanted a devotional that was strong on God's Word. I wanted more than a verse a day. I wanted more than a few paragraphs that someone else had written *about* the Bible. I wanted the Bible.

147

So, we developed the BIBS devotional book—a daily and weekly study through various books of the Bible. The BIBS devotional book is a simple notebook with daily checklists. You read, reread, and flag words on certain days and work to interpret Scripture the other days. After spending a day or two in a text, you apply the truth and move to a new text the next day. Each day, in addition to the interpretation, you reread the entire chapter (or more) in order to keep you in the overall flow of the text.

This format of devotional provides both the depth of Scripture as well as keeping in mind the overall concepts (simultaneous interpretation and observation).

Once my wife fully grasped the concepts taught in this book, the Bible came alive to her. For a summary and excerpt from the BIBS Devotional book, please see Appendix 3.

Daily Bible Reading

A second way to use the BIBS format, beyond the BIBS devotional, is to use it as a simple structure in your daily Bible reading. If you use a Bible reading schedule, consider adding the BIBS process to your daily quiet time.

Completing the Bible in a year requires reading three or four chapters per day. If you are following the one-year plan, consider focusing on one text (perhaps 3-4 verses) and put it through the BIBS process. Read, reread, flag words, boil it down to a word, expand it to a phrase, expand to a sentence, turn it into a question and answer it, applying the truth afterwards.

For both deep and wide study, one day you could breeze through the text to get a wide overview. The next day, you could reread the same text and focus in on one shorter text.

Think of one or every text like this. If you learn to discipline your thinking in this way, you will learn to always think of the Bible as a message from God. Every time you read a verse you will think, "I wonder what God is trying to tell me right now."

Lessons

A third way to use the BIBS process is to write sermons, object lessons, devotions, class lessons or any other type of lesson where you might be sharing God's Word with others. You might be asked to preach in church or you might be giving a devotion in the cabin at summer camp. You might be visiting a retirement center or giving a class speech on ancient literature.

You can use the BIBS process to come up with a truth, apply it to yourself, and then share with others how it helped you. (Here's a hint: that is what preachers and Bible teachers do every week. At least, that is what they SHOULD do.)

Everyday Truth

A fourth way to use the BIBS process is to let it change your thinking about everyday truth. All truth is God's truth, and every truthful principle in life has its roots in Scripture.

No matter what happens in life, good or bad, consider the circumstance in light of God's Word. As you learn to hear from God every day through His Word, the lens through which you view the world will slowly change for the better.

Everyday life becomes biblical life when seen through the truth of God's Word. I pray BIBS helps in your biblical and spiritual growth.

APPENDICES

Appendix 1

Genres - A Deeper Review

You Don't Even Have To Read This Stuff

Chapter 5 gave the overview of some of the biblical genres and their definitions. It also provided examples of where the genres are used in the Bible. Appendix 1 is an expansion on those thoughts, arranged in no particular order and grouped by genre.

Appendix 1 is written very academically. It is good bedtime reading material as it will easily put you to sleep. Appendix 1 is meant solely for reference material and a clearer definition of each topic. You don't even have to read this chapter. It's too boring.

So, in no particular order, enjoy:

Law

Summary: *This contains the instructions and precepts of Moses, such as Leviticus and Deuteronomy. Law is "God's law", and is the expression of His sovereign will and character. The writings of Moses contain a lot of Law. God provided the Jews with many laws (619 or so). These laws defined the proper relationship with God, to one another, and with the world (the alien), as well as for worshipping God, governing the people, priestly duties, what to eat and not eat, how to build the temple, proper behavior, manners, and social interaction, etc. The Ten Commandments are often known as "The Law;" so are Exodus, Leviticus, Numbers, and Deuteronomy. In the New Testament, the "Sermon on the Mount" is considered law and the fulfillment of the law, and Paul's calls to the church are law in their literature form.*

Most Christians have a distorted view of the law and think it does not apply to us. Jesus repeated and affirmed the Ten Commandments and the Law of Moses. The law points to our depravity and need for a Savior. Without the law, there would be no relationship to God or need for Christ to save us. Christ fulfills the law and thus we are not bound to its curse, but we must acknowledge its role in our lives as the pointer to the cross and the mirror to our soul.

Introduction

The law in general is a theme found throughout all of Scripture, whether in the times before Moses, or when penned at Sinai, or when found in the New Testament. Though God's thoughts on sin, on right, and on wrong have never changed, the culture and issues around us have changed, and God's dealings with man have changed as well. Certain laws that are laid out in the Old Testament have puzzled scholars and lesser-learned believers alike, and some answers have been sought sometimes to no avail. While God does not want us to be confused, at the same time there is no question that some of the rituals and ceremonies are not for today, but which ones? And why? And why did they have to do them? These and other questions are explored in this chapter.

How Law and Genre Analysis Are Related

To fully realize and comprehend the laws, how they related then and how they relate now, one cannot but examine the cultures and settings in which they were written—being genre-sensitive. The purpose of this is simply to understand what is really going on, and what the point of the text really is. But without looking at the entire scope is to miss the boat completely. The focus of this chapter is on the law penned by Moses, and one cannot examine this portion of the law without first understanding the terms *covenant, law,* and *ritual legislation.*

How a Covenant Functions

Four major covenants are found in Scripture—the Abrahamic covenant, the Mosaic covenant, the Davidic covenant, and the new covenant. The influence of these four covenants are seen throughout the pages of Scripture, and are more than just contracts, but are binding relationships over long periods of time. The covenant in the wilderness was almost a corporate account of the one on one covenant between Jacob and Laban. In the case of the relationship between God and Israel, the Lord first proposed the covenant, "Israel then proclaimed their anticipatory acceptance of the covenant... the Lord declared the stipulations of the covenant," and Israel agreed to it (the stipulations) by being "deeply committed on an individual and corporate level to living that way before him (the oath)."[1]

How Law Functions

The law functions within the boundaries, protection, provision, and scope of the covenant in which it is set. It is as if the covenant is the frame, and the law is the canvas—made more beautiful and more readily seen with the frame around it. At the same time, the law is set into the relationship of the Mosaic covenant, and the limits of the law and its applications are found only within the bounds of the covenant. "God expects the people whom he has redeemed...to take their covenant commitment seriously...because he takes his covenant commitment to them seriously..."[2] These laws given by God are basically divided into two groups: apodictic—"unconditionally and categorically assert right and wrong"[3]—and case or casuistic—"laws that define specific cases and prescribed legal consequences."[4] While the latter is very cut and dry, the former has more of a moral background, and is bound less by culture and time. Studies have further divided each category, and even some have taken it too far in certain areas. The study is simply to help us understand better what is being said.

How Ritual Legislation Functions

These passages containing ritual legislation can be considered a subgenre of the law, and act in a way that contributes to the whole. These rituals applied more to the priestly functions, and included the foundation for all that took place in the religious world. The cleansing of that which was unclean in those days took place through rituals and ceremonies. This purification process had different stages and intensities required, but all of it pointed to the physical presence of the Lord with them at all times. Regular, irregular, and severe uncleanness each required different levels of cleansing, sometimes even expulsion from the camp, but all served toward not only cleansing not only the tabernacle, but the whole community as well.

How Old Testament Law Applies to Christians

This has been a question for decades. There really are no definite lines given in Scripture, but we know from the New Testament that Christ did come to fulfill the law. In doing so he took the law actually to a whole new level—even higher and more personally accountable! While certain aspects of the old law still apply directly, the ceremonial and ritual laws do not. What does apply is that now we are to love God and love our neighbors—enveloping the whole law in two commandments. We see the sacrificial laws, for example, as pictures of how we should now present our lives since we are Christians.

Where Legal Literature Is Found in the East

Covenant. The Hittite treaties found in ancient writings contained many of the same (if not identical) aspects as the above-mentioned "steps" made in what we know as a covenant. These treaties, loyalty oaths, and royal grants differed in relationships, but the idea is similar in that it was an agreement between two.

Law. Similar in function, though not followed to the letter as the Israelites were supposed to, the laws of the ancient Babylonians and others sought to simply "preserve law and order as a living and continuing tradition."5 These Mesopotamian laws included comparisons and contrasts, but were not a clear-cut, perfect example and parallel to the biblical law—though lessons could be gleaned from them.

Ritual Legislations. The pagan priests had rules for cleaning and offering their sacrifices, and parallels are again drawn here, though not perfect representations, because, of course, many differences abound.

How to Interpret Law

1. Observe the context within the canon.
2. Note the style of the law—apodictic or case law; subgenres.
3. Examine the grammar of the law.
4. Compare laws in the biblical text with one another.
5. Look for parallels with the ancient Near East literature. [But be careful here]
6. Seek to determine the meaning of words, phrases, clauses, sentences, and paragraphs. 6

Conclusion

Studying the law is a study of relationships, not rites and rules. This relationship has expectations on one end, and "tangible expressions of that bond" on the other. We today are meant to study it in the correct light, rather than with our own cultural filters, in order to glean the most from it, and in order to preach, teach, and apply it as the Lord intended.

- 1 Page 119
- 2 Page 119
- 3 Page 120
- 4 Page 120
- 5 Page 128
- 6 Pages 130-131

History or Narrative

Summary: *These are the stories and the epics, and include: Genesis, Exodus, Numbers, Joshua, Judges, Ruth, 1 and 2 Samuel, 1 and 2 Kings, 1 and 2 Chronicles, Ezra, Nehemiah, Esther, Jonah, and Acts. Almost every Old Testament book contains history. Some books of the Bible are grouped together and commonly referred to as the "History" (Joshua, Kings, and Chronicles); these books tell us the history of the Jewish people from the time of the Judges through the Persian Empire. In the New Testament, Acts contains some of the history of the early church, and the Gospels also have history; Jesus' life is told as history. Even the Epistles have history as they chronicle events. Another sub-category of narrative is called romance. This is narrative written also as a love story such as Ruth and Song of Solomon.*

NARRATIVE – Introduction

We all enjoy a good story, and have all learned from a story, whether good or bad. A narrative is a biblical truth wrapped up in a story form, and rarely is that truth ever explicitly brought to light. It is through the effects and principles found within the different aspects and details of a story that God chose to relate to us some of the truths He wanted us to know. He as our Creator and Sustainer knows what we like, how we learn, and what works for us, and though He is not here to please us, He used stories—narratives—to illustrate and thereby teach us much of what we know of Him. Rather than

158

straight propositions and precepts for us to swallow and simply accept, (though there is a bit of that in the Scriptures), God allowed it that we can relate, empathize, understand, and experience His truth through a story He has written for us that will stand through time. Generations have passed on traditions, beliefs, and rights through stories, and though we are not into this "Religious Experience" movement, we cannot deny the fact that a story lived in the imagination's eye is a strong teacher—more powerful than almost any other realm of learning.

What are the Components of a Narrative?

Like a recipe, a story is made up of different parts, and all these parts work together as a whole to create the essence, feel, and ultimately the true meaning of a story. Scholars have come up with these different aspects, and they are as follows: scene, plot, point of view, characterization, setting, dialogue, structural levels, and stylistic or rhetorical devices.

Scene

First, the most important aspect is the scene of the story or event—what happened, what was said, who said it, and details of the situation as a whole. Most scenes consist of two characters or groups of characters, and many times God is directly or indirectly one of the main characters. After all, the Bible is given to us to reveal Him, and it is our job to analyze the Scriptures and find out what He is conveying through His Word. A look at the scene and the different areas of the scene will help us do just that.

Plot

Without a plot—a storyline—a tale has no meaning. In the realms of Scripture, it has no truth or validity. A plot in a story is the sequence of events that hold attention and at the same time teach a lesson. As the plot unfolds throughout the pages, usually present is a scenario of some sort of conflict, a gradual rise of tension, a climax, and finally a recession; only to usually repeat the cycle once again. The pace can either be accelerated or dragged on, depending on details and intent, but all narratives will have a beginning, a middle, and an end. It is an examination of the whole that leads to correct interpretation.

B.I.B.S. - Big Idea Bible Study

Point of View

From what side, and from what aspect is the author writing? What is his perspective? Four points of view emerge to interpret narratives in the Bible: spatial, temporal, psychological, and ideological. With *spatial*, a character is "chosen" and details of his life are examined without knowing the details of others around him. *Temporal* entails the storyline and no more, while *psychological* enters into the mind, thoughts, and feelings of the character involved. Lastly, *ideology* refers to the evaluations, estimations, and analysis of the author on the text—ultimately ordained by God. Each point of view serves as a guide along the way.

Characterization

Details in the Scriptures are not spurious whims created by the author in order to draw us in to the story; details furnished by the Holy Spirit have so much more meaning than that, and so ought to require diligent attention. Usually if a certain detail is given, the reason for it comes out in the story at a later time.

Also, characters are often contrasted against one another—details against details and whole against whole. The characters of the Bible are categorized in three ways: round, flat, or as an agent. I cannot put it better than Sandy and Giese: "A round character has many traits, is more complex, and therefore less predictable, but more real. A flat character usually only has one trait and thus is single-dimensional. An agent has no personality at all, but simply functions to move the story along."

Setting

Important to the interpretation of a narrative is the setting in which it is held. The events surrounding the scene, the dates and location of the story serve to give the story life, validity, and reference for later study and cross-reference.

Dialogue

As mentioned before, details about a biblical character are somewhat rare in a sense, but facts about a person's life can often be deduced from the content of the dialogue between them and another. Notice two rules given by Alter in *The Art of Biblical Narrative*, p. 182: "Note the place where the dialogue is first being introduced, for that will be an important moment in revealing the character of the speaker—perhaps even more than in the substance of what is said. Note also where the narrator has chosen to introduce dialogue instead of narration." The contrasts found by following these rules will help in determining the meaning of the text, and finding the dialogue will point you to know that you are dealing with a biblical narrative.

Structural Level

Definition: "...Structures that are a network of relations among the parts of an object or a unit."

Stylistic or Rhetorical Devices

Each text has a style to it, or sometimes a combination of styles, and is dependent on five areas that the author may have decided to use: repetition, omission, inclusion, chiasm, and irony. Repetition is how often a word, phrase, or thought is used, and until recently has been overlooked as to its importance and emphasis in Scripture. Omission has been used almost at the discretion of the author, in that the story only included that which was necessary in order to relay the meaning of the passage. Inclusion draws emphasis that may have been lacking, and chiasm is a linguistic term for switching or inverting words or elements in a text. Irony is used in Scripture and has been in literature all through the ages, and is another tool. Caution must be taken, in that irony must be interpreted with the author's intent in mind, without making ironic what was not intended, and without digging deeper than was meant, finding deeper meanings and stretching the irony to *all* parts of a story. All these aspects are simply tools to guide and assist in our next section, interpreting narrative.

Interpreting Narrative

Though principles of interpretation sometimes change, certain foundational guidelines can be held that will transcend time.

1. *Identify each scene of the narrative.* Summarize the words and thoughts of the author.

161

2. *Analyze the plot of the narrative.* Notice the beginning, middle, climax, and end of the story.

3. Determine the point of view from which the narrative is recorded.

4. Pay close attention to the details of the scene. Find significance in everything possible.

5. *Examine the dialogue* that the author uses to narrate the story.

6. *Look at the units* within a scene and their relationship with one another.

7. *Study the stylistic devices the author used:* repetition, omission, inclusion, chiasm, irony, and others.

Conclusion

All too often, conclusions about the meaning of a passage of the infinite Word of God have been made without proper attention given to the proper means of interpreting His Word. Christians are too soon guilty of wresting the Scriptures as a means to make it say what they want it to say. It is a sin to ignore the true teachings of God. Application can be made, and aspects in a story might relate to some aspects today, but it is the true meaning—the central idea or theme of a text—that we are after. Only after we find that timeless truth that God meant to convey in the first place should application be made. Biblical narrative is an exciting genre, and should be studied as intended by God.

HISTORY – Introduction

History. His story. The very name describes this genre. It is a genre of writing that is used nearly every day for every person alive. The term *history* can be used to describe the ancient study; it can be used to describe the details of yesterday, or it can even be used to describe the second that just passed as you read this sentence. History is simply the account of what has taken place from a person's perspective, but a more detailed look at events and people of the past to determine their position and impact on civilization is what experts call historiography. Biblical history is no different in form from the history that we know today, although its contents are what separate it from the rest. It is the living Word of God, and thus it's inspired pages are "a historical record of the outworking of divine intention and purpose in human affairs."[1] The bulk of the history that is found in the Scripture is found in the first half of the Old Testament, and requires careful interpretation.

What Makes History Different from Narrative?

While history does contain the aspects of narrative storytelling, (and many other genres for that matter), the difference lies in the fact that stories tend to be more emotional and open to embellishment where history is more of a statement of facts. History is a major part of the Old Testament, and relies heavily upon storytelling to create interest; at the same time it is completely true. Though the two seem to be nearly identical, history is *national* rather than familial or tribal, and is simply used for records instead of stories, though stories are a *means* of recordkeeping.

Also, history is simply a recounting of "a series of accounts...with cause-effect sequences given much more weight than a plot. History is a tapestry of accounts in which there is a place for each account and each account in its place." It is generally more noted by commentary—the author interjecting thoughts or feelings on the discussed subject—than narrative is, and God is more often portrayed as being represented through a man, rather than openly speaking as He would normally in a narrative.

How History Functions

The Samuels, Kings, and Chronicles have served as somewhat of a template for historical accounts throughout the Bible. The Samuels have been simply a "history of the succession of the throne of David,"[2] and are made up of numerous sub-genres that contribute to the whole.

The account of 1 and 2 Kings declares the history of the nations of Israel and Judah, their successive kings and prophets, the details of the thrones, and the stories of the people involved from Solomon to the exiled Jehoiachin. Narrative is a major part of this historical account, but numerous sub-genres are again found in this text as well—over two dozen are listed. The author says that "recognition of these literary devices and forms and how they contribute to the historical narrative is crucial to the hermeneutical and theological study of Kings."[3]

Lastly, The Chronicles serve as simply a recapitulation of the time period (and more) already covered in Samuel and Kings, (copies of which the author of Chronicles may have had before him as he wrote), and is simply another aspect of the same picture. Though different from the Hebrew annals—a year-by-year account of the happenings and major instances—it could easily be confused. The Chronicles are more than a concise collection of events, and are a selection of accounts not in any particular order. The genres enlisted are among the same as the above, and as a whole the Chronicles are in writing to "tell how Israel is organized and thereby who and what it is."[4]

Is History in the Old Testament Unique?

Many countries in the Middle East at the time of the writing of the Bible had a form of history unique to them, in that the had accounts of days gone by, battles won, and kingship conquests etcetera; but only Greece and Israel had a written form of history that is known today. The old Egyptian pharaohs would trace in their writing the accomplishments of their lives on the walls of tombs, but even that was sporadic at best and did not serve as a cohesive unit that can be studied as history. The people of Egypt and Mesopotamia did, however, make an impact on the Israelites in causing their history to be written.

Questions About the Accuracy of Historical Narrative

The question of authenticity has arisen due to a number of factors, not the least of which is the difficulty in understanding the chronology (or lack of it) in the historical accounts. Though our minds are used to thinking in that way, the method of the ancient biblical writers "has nothing to do with the credibility of the accounts but only with their understanding."[5] The point is not whether we understand the events in their order in time, but whether we understand the message that the biblical author intends to communicate through time. Objectivity is definitely present, but does not represent a message or facts that are not correct.

Several questions can be asked to "test" the ideology and/or theology of historical narratives. Is the narrator interjecting his own beliefs on the story? How far in detail does the author go on a particular person compared to other accounts? (A question of emphasis, not truth.) How much truth is simply a further or restating of previously known facts or truths? The over-arching theological concern should be greater than the supposed differences.

Questions about the accuracy have arisen because of the embellishment of authors. To reply, historians will tell you that a bit of embellishment is actually necessary, due to the fact that the authors were not usually eye-witnesses, and had a freedom to do so in order to make the story come alive. As a literary technique, it is brilliant, and as a contradiction to inspiration it is unfounded. Each gospel account was the story from one author's perspective, including his twist on the story and the dialogue used. Each is every bit inspired, and the same is for the historical accounts.

How to Interpret Historical Literature

Guidelines

1. Determine the scope of the historical narrative under consideration. Put the story in its overall context, and build from there.
2. *Recognize that the historical record is only that—a record and not the event itself.* Readers must be sensitive to how an event is recorded and interpreted in written form.
3. *Look for evidence of the author's purpose in recording the story.* It is not a statement of facts, but a deeper meaning is behind and under every account.
4. *Examine the features of historical narrative carefully* for the meaning that is usually implicit rather than explicit.
5. *Do not suppose that what happened in a historical narrative is a prescriptive for what should happen.* Illustrations are given of good and bad examples, and what we want the Bible to say is not the issue—the issue is what the Bible says, discovered through these and other steps.

6. Permit the details in historical narratives simply to be supporting facts for the main point of the story. Do not try to allegorize every aspect of the story when they are only supposed to serve the whole.

7. *Do not look for devotional or doctrinal content in every historical narrative.* Though there is meaning to every word written, sometimes a step back to get a look at the whole picture is needed. The point is...read a little more.

1 Merrill, (Sandy and Giese), p. 89

2 Ibid, p. 92

3 Ibid, p. 95

4 Ibid, p. 97

5 Ibid, p. 102

Wisdom

Summary: This is the literature of maxims and sayings, including Job, Proverbs, and Ecclesiastes. Wisdom Literature focuses on questions about the meaning of life (Job, Ecclesiastes) and on practical living and common sense (Proverbs and some Psalms). This literature contrasts our faulty human wisdom to God's reasoning perfection. Thus, when we live for our own will and not His, we will experience grief and frustration, not because God is vengeful and angry, but because we led ourselves that way out of our pride and arrogance. This literature warns us of our evil nature and desires.

Poetry

Summary: These are the prose and rhyme books such as Psalms, Song of Solomon, and Lamentations. Poetry is found mostly in the Old Testament and is similar to modern poetry. Since it is a different language of Hebrew, the Bible's poetry can be very different because it does not translate into

166

English very well. Poetry that we are used to is usually based on parallelisms, rhythm, or various types of sound mixings, as is our music. Hebrew poetry is based on a tempo of stanzas and phrases re-told differently called "synonymous parallelism," conveying the same ideas and meaning in contrasting or similar ways. Some called "synthetic parallelism," also have extra ideas and words inserted. "Antithetic parallelism" is mostly contrasting stanzas, and is very predominant in Proverbs. Some Bible books are all poetry (Psalms, Song of Songs, and Lamentations), and some books only have a few verses such as in Luke.

Gospel

Summary: This word means the "good news" that we received through salvation by the work and life of God's Son, Jesus Christ. When the Gospels were first written in the first century, it was a brand new form of literature. The four Gospels (Mark, Matthew, Luke, and John) contain a bit of all the literary types with the primary purpose of expressing faith in Christ and what He has done on our behalf. In these works, the stories are not necessarily in chronological or sequential order, except for Luke. In this type of literature, we find what is called a parable. These are the sayings of Jesus that are narrative and instructional, contained in the Gospels. Each of the gospels presents the teachings, ministry, death, and resurrection of Jesus in a distinctive way, but not contradictory, and for a specific audience. Matthew was written to Jews, and Luke to Greeks, both with different ways of reasoning and thinking. Think of the Gospels like the facets of a diamond, giving more depth and meaning.

Parables

Summary: These are the sayings of Jesus told in a short story or illustration form that are narrative and instructional; they teach a truth, and are contained in the Gospels. Usually, these are from everyday life examples that may have taken place or may not. At times, such as in the

Parable of the Sower, Jesus was possibly pointing to it as He taught. These had a deeper purpose than the face value of the illustration, thus it took some thinking and a desire to learn in order to understand them. Perhaps, He used them to keep people of impiety and without intent of faith from bothering Him; or, perhaps He wanted to challenge the skeptics and people who were unresponsive.

Epistle

Summary: This refers to the 21 letters in the New Testament written to a specific audience that are also practical for us today such as Romans, Corinthians, Galatians, Ephesians, Philippians, Colossians, Thessalonians, Timothy, Titus, Philemon, Hebrews, James, Peter, John, and the first three chapters of Revelation. Epistles are the personal letters from the Apostles to their churches. These letters are both different and similar to the letters of their time. Most challenge the congregation to wake up out of their selfish ways and to concentrate on Christ in specific ways and clarifications. They begin with the names of the writer and the recipient, then a greeting, a reason for the letter, and then the central message or body of the letter; there is usually a closing, just like most letters today.

The epistles deal with concerns and false teachings that needed immediate correction. Some epistles were written in response to questions from the church, or for clarification for another letter, such as II Corinthians. The teachings of the epistles applied to both to the church they were written to, and also to Christians today. However, we need to understand the cultural and historical situation to better understand what is going on, so we do not misunderstand what is being said.

Prophecy

Summary: Prophecy means past, present, and future, not just the future. This includes major and minor prophets—Isaiah, Jeremiah, Ezekiel, Daniel,

Hosea, Joel, Amos, Obadiah, Micah, Nahum, Habakkuk, Zephaniah, Haggai, Zechariah, and Malachi. Prophecy is the type of literature that is often associated with predicting the future. However, it also contains God's words of "get with it, or else…" There are two main types. One is "predictive," as in foretelling an event, and the other is "didactic," challenging others to line up morally or to teach a truth. Thus, prophecy also exposes sin and calls for repentance and obedience. It shows how God's law can be applied to specific problems and situations, such as the repeated warnings to the Jews before their captivity. This is found in the Old Testament books of Isaiah through Malachi, the section of the Bible labeled "Prophecy" by both Jews and Christians. There are over 2,000 specific predictions that have already come to pass, hundreds of years after the author's death!

In the New Testament, prophecy is mainly found in Matthew 24 and the book of Revelation. Prophecy has both an immediate call to a given situation, such as the "seven churches of Revelation," and a predated future to come to pass. That is, it is two fold—a past and a future, both applying to the present. Some predictions are already fulfilled, such as the birth, life, death, and resurrection of Jesus Christ and some have yet to come to pass such as sections of Daniel, 2 Peter, Revelation, and the return of Christ.

Apocalyptic

Summary: *These are combinations of narrative and prose written in vivid imagery and poetic phrases that are intended for a purpose such as Daniel and most of Revelation. Apocalyptic writing is a more specific form of prophecy, and is a type of literature that warns us of future events. Apocalyptic writing is found in Isaiah, Daniel, Ezekiel, Zechariah, and Revelation.*

Introduction

People much smarter than I have stated that the most difficult genre to study and understand is apocalyptic, and due to its nature I would tend to agree. Many have tried to twist, pervert, or maybe only have misunderstood this almost-prophetic language, but if it is understood, it can be one of the most elating studies that a person can do. For a biblical author to portray a feeling rather than simply pour out facts is a beautiful feat, and for our minds to grasp a picture rather than a flat statement is what our programmed minds yearn for. The beauty of pictorial language, the majesty of description, and the emotion of learning through the experience-dominated side of our brains is quite a thought, and for an author to express all of *that* in mere words is no nominal task—it is an artist's craft. Apocalyptic writing ravishes in all the splendor of almost every colorful literary technique known.

What Makes Apocalyptic Unique?

How is it different from prophecy? Though the answer to that is not black and white, a few guidelines have been made in observation of both genres.

PROPHECY	APOCALYPTIC
Laments the sinfulness on the earth and urges people to repent.	Considers the ever-present wickedness beyond hope. The only solution is total destruction: The earth is going to melt with fervent heat.
Reveals God's displeasure with the irreverent attitudes and conduct of his chosen people.	Assumes that the readers are themselves displeased with the evil around them and are anxious for God to provide a solution.

Calls the people of God back to obedience to God.	Calls for the few remaining faithful to persevere until the end: In the face of difficult odds they are to keep their robes pure.
Announces that God is going to judge sin and offer salvation, usually to be accomplished through natural means or human agents.	Announces that God himself is going to intervene and judge the world through supernatural means: he will ride out of heaven on a white horse and rule the nations.
Presents its message as direct speech from God: "Thus saith the Lord."	Presents its message in graphic images, visions, and symbols. The message of apocalyptic is sometimes shrouded in mystery: "And upon her forehead was a name written, MYSTERY, BABYLON THE GREAT, THE MOTHER OF HARLOTS AND ABOMINATIONS OF THE EARTH." Rev 17:5
Predicts both immediate and distant aspects of God's judgment and salvation.	Focuses primarily on final solutions. The situation is too serious for short-term answers. The only hope is for God to bring the history of man's sinfulness to conclusion and to establish a solution that will last for eternity: There will be no more night, and they will reign for ever and ever.

To the reader, the figurative language in apocalyptic may seem strange, but it is all in order to bring about one final purpose—to offer hope.

Where Apocalyptic is Found

Extra-Biblical Writings. As mentioned, it is difficult to establish a set of rules for understanding this genre, and when a series of underlying factors necessary has been set, no biblical passage can be found to fill every set of rules. Therefore, other sources may have similarities in some areas, and widely differ in others—the point is that some books outside of the Bible offer insights and shed light on the Bible in that culture. Most of the writings which are apocalyptic in nature are in the Pseudopigrapha, but other writings were found and date all the way back to around 1000 BC! These and others can contribute, but must never take place or determine the interpreting of the Bible.

Old Testament Writings. Much of the Old Testament includes at least traces of the genre, and many of the prophets shifted from a message of judgment, and included a message of hope in this apocalyptic form. Daniel is one of the most widely known and recognized with the pictures representing future nations and such, as well as Ezekiel's description of Gog and Magog. Also Joel, Zechariah, and Malachi contain future implications relating to this idea.

How Apocalyptic Functions

The idea of apocalyptic as a whole is this: to offer hope in time of trouble. Often, the people would be so overwhelmed in their sin, in their trials, in their judgments, or in their daily lives that they would forget what the big picture was really all about, and this genre, with all its related passages, is to get the people to view their miniscule problems in the grand scheme of things. It was and is a clever and magnanimous way to get our eyes off ourselves and back on to God.

How to Interpret Apocalyptic Literature

Once again, one cannot interpret this from his own general reading, but one must understand the text from the original standpoint—What was the biblical author trying to get across to his readers *at that time?* There is simply no other way around it, but still many try to twist Scripture to their ideas.

1. Study biblical apocalyptic in the light of apocalyptic ways of thinking in the ancient world.
2. Read apocalyptic in view of a context of crisis. It is a source of encouragement.
3. Do not look for something in apocalyptic that it does not intend to disclose. Though apocalyptic authors do have something important to communicate, it is more hope for the future than information about the future
4. Expect apocalyptic to be full of metaphorical language.
5. Do not attempt to identify the significance of every detail of apocalyptic. This may leave the significance of some portions of an apocalypse a mystery.
6. Keep all options open for how apocalyptic predictions will be fulfilled.
7. Seek to understand the main point of an apocalyptic text. Apocalyptic tends to be impressionistic, more like an abstract painting that communicates an overall impression.
8. Appreciate the full and rich symbolism of apocalyptic.

Conclusion

The textbook author again spells out line by line the judgment of Gog. This ultimately spells out that the apocalyptic nature is to offer hope. Plain and simple. The encouragement and hope is to persevere to the end.

Oracles of Salvation

Introduction

Though it comes under the guise of many other themes—forgiveness of sin, justification, sanctification, and deliverance from difficulties—salvation is the binding factor of the entire Bible, and offers hope in many different ways.

173

Salvation is a theme of promise, blessing, and salvation, and all themes work together in order to form what we know as the canon of Scripture in all its majesty.

This word *salvation* is composed of a few different aspects. First, promise has been mentioned in correlation with other genres, and is seen especially in the Old Testament. We have seen it in the covenant between God and his people, and it is simply the assurance of God's deliverance in the face of all obstacles. Secondly, the idea of blessing comes with salvation. It is a general promise that obedience will bring about the well-being, and profit of the one obeying. Basic needs will be met, in home life, personal comfort, and general life as well. These blessings come in both a present and a future sense, and the hope of resurrection and future enjoyment in heaven bring an added highlight to the blessings promised.

The word *salvation* carries a few different ideas, as discussed, and the oracles are simply the proclaiming of those ideas. God speaks through a man, and the man addresses individuals or nations with a sense of comfort and/or deliverance in a time of need.

What Makes Oracles of Salvation Unique

The "first-fruits" of the oracles of salvation are found a lot in Genesis, and the beginning stages are often good times. The oracles of salvation in later years, however (after some of the promises have been fulfilled and others have been breached by the people of God), are a bit different in the prophets. These oracles are intertwined in the oracles of judgment. In times of trouble and running, the people are both warned of impending doom, but are at the same time reassured that there will be an end, and a reward for obedience to the Lord.

The *messenger formula* is a term used to define the authority with which a prophet speaks, in that he is not speaking something of his own, rather he is speaking what the Lord says to speak. The phrase often seen is "Thus saith the Lord..." to open up an oracle from God, whether an oracle of salvation or judgment as well. Another term is *a word of salvation*. This is more of an encouraging word in a time of trouble, and correlates with the oracles of salvation in more of a positive way—with a reassurance of God's presence, an answer to prayer, or such else.

The written oracles differed from the prophets of older time, such as Elijah, in that the judgment and salvation oracles were written down and usually given to a corporate nation, rather than an individual like a king or national leader. An important point to notice here is that rather than a moment deciding the point of salvation, with the written prophets the revelation is more of a process and is revealed over a period of time.

Two subgenres also come to light in the oracles of salvation, with the *promise of salvation* referring to a corporate nation as more like an individual, such as God referring to Israel as a single person. The second subgenre is the *proclamation of salvation*, and is usually in response to that communal repentance—usually a lament. In summary, oracles of salvation are simply a reassuring word from God that he will bless and help those who are obedient in time of need. The messenger formula often introduces it, and the blessing comes in many forms—salvation from enemies, personal joy or fulfillment, or a renewed fellowship with God, to name a few.

Where Oracles of Salvation Are Found

Though we do not put much clout in the extra-biblical sources, nor do we use them to prove the Bible correct, they can help us to determine some time frames, and help us understand the biblical accounts a little bit better. Many of the letters of the ancient Near East include some of the same wordings and ideas as we see in the oracles of salvation of the Bible, where the idea of "fear not" can be seen throughout much of the writings. Also seen is the idea of blessings, but more toward the individual (usually kings) rather than the nation as we see with Israel.

How to Interpret Oracles of Salvation

1. *Be sensitive to the prophetic imagery.* Sometimes these scenes may seem strange to the casual reader, but not always does a prophet come out and say, "Thus saith the Lord..." Often, the oracle comes

through a promise of a stream in the desert, a new land, or an abandoned fortress—all imagery to show a future judgment or a future deliverance and restoration of Israel. The themes of both judgment and restoration come in this image-based speaking.

2. *Relate the assurances of promise and blessing to God's previous commitments made with creation, Abraham, Moses, and David.* Remember, all oracles of salvation are somewhat tied to other passages, particularly the origins of the promises. Each of the men mentioned in the opening sentence here were given a promise, Israel was to carry out the promise, almost always Israel failed, judgment would come, and then an oracle of salvation would be incorporated into the judgment, all because of the original promise.

3. *Examine the dual background of the exile and restoration of the exiles to the land.* This salvation to the people in exile partially meant that one day they would be able to return to their promised land, and the words of comfort came when they were assured of this very fact. The exile was due to their disobedience and was meant for them to return back to the Father in humility and repentance, but not without hope of future protection.

4. *Interpret the prophetic oracles from the perspective of transformation.* All involved will be transformed at a future time, including not only the people, but the leadership and the earth as well. The people will be a humble people in the new era, according to the Bible, and the leadership will be under the "Child-King, a descendant of David."

5. *Understand the fulfillment of oracles as a process.* Mentioned earlier, over time, the revelation of God becomes more and more clear. Fulfillment is more of a process, and less of an event.

6. *Ask what response the prophet was eliciting.* Not only did the prophet desire to assure the people of a future blessing, but he was also pushing toward an immediate change. The free gift of their salvation was without strings, yes, but it took an effort to obey on their part in order to partake in the blessing.

7. *Look for the complete fulfillment of the oracles of salvation in the coming of Jesus.* The blessings are present, but the entire fulfilling of all the promises will not come to pass until the new kingdom is ushered in.

Conclusion

One author includes a step-by-step guide through the interpreting of the prophecies of Jeremiah, and points out that the message that was a burden on his heart was by no means just a message of judgment, but mixed in was the oracles of salvation of which we have been speaking this whole time. Almost all 7 of the different aspects we mentioned above are present in this view, and for a "hands on" look, he included his findings. In conclusion, God sees and cares, and desires for us to be with him. We see this as fragments of mercy mixed in with judgment, and view all the judgment as a way to draw closer to Him.

Announcements of Judgment

Introduction

The message of God came loud and clear in those days. He used means that He does not use today, and He had an agenda that is not necessarily up-to-date in our peanut brains. He had a plan for the children of Israel, He clearly laid the guidelines, the people transgressed, or went outside the bounds, and for this they would be punished. This is not to say that the Lord is not longsuffering—conversely, He was so longsuffering that he allowed hundreds of years of figurative back-stabbing, and still loved and tried to help them. He put up with their moaning and groaning throughout their entire history, and when we would have wiped them off the face of the earth, had we been God, He allowed them to continue on. He sent messages and messengers time and time again, and yet at times more drastic measures were needed. At these times, God would separate a man, commission him, equip him with a message, and command him to deliver it to the people. It is these messages that we read about a lot through the Old Testament, and they are messages or warning, judgment, discipline, and punishment—none were taken well by the people, and the method in delivering the message is a unique study.

How the Prophets Proclaimed the Message from God

As mentioned above, the prophet had a message from God, but he used special methods in relaying this message—methods that had to transform the people's thinking about their sin. Two ideas have come from two different sources, and they are summarized simply in the response desired. First, did God desire for the people to change their behavior? Or second, was He simply instructing them of the doom to follow? The answer to each of those questions depends on the text, and one cannot jump to conclusions about what the biblical author was trying to convey without careful study.

How Announcements of Judgment Function

In man, an emotional aspect is built into even the most hardened individual, and the emotional side of the intellect needs to be won over before the person can accept anything as fact. I say that to say this: the prophets had to overcome one of the hardest obstacles—the people's emotions about their sin. To do this a variety of means were used, and really are still used in different aspects today. You see, a king in those days would send a messenger to speak on his behalf to another foreign court, and the prophet was acting just like that messenger. He was to dictate verbatim what the king had said, and then explain the message. The prophet was one who would deliver the message with an introduction like "Thus saith the Lord..." declare the judgment succinctly, and then proceed to expound on the judgment, i.e. with reasons for the judgment.

One form of proclaiming this prophetic message was through the *woe article*—a direct calling out of what was being done wrongly by the individual. It was a no-nonsense approach that got right to the heart of the matter and pronounced outright judgment, naming the sin and the sinners. This woe oracle consisted of the grieving woe article, and then the description or the reasons for the woe, detailing the transgression.

"The *prophetic lawsuit* summons Israel to court to hear God's verdict. This has five parts:

1. An introduction calling the audience to hear and often appealing to heavens and earth as witness
2. Questioning of witnesses and statement of the accusation

3. The prosecuting attorney's address to the court contrasting the people's sins with God's saving acts
4. Description of the inability of cultic ritual to atone for such wrong acts
5. A warning and a call to turn back to God and obey Him."[1]

A third form is the *summons to repentance,* which is often debated by scholars, but deals with whether God is simply informing the people of their transgressions and thus their punishment for them, or whether He is giving them a choice to repent and turn from their wicked ways in order to avoid the judgment and punishment for past sins. "The prophet uses the following elements:

• An appeal using messenger formula, vocative, and admonition; and
• A motivation with promise, accusation and threat."[2]

Where Announcements of Judgment Are Found

As mentioned in previous articles, no extra-biblical sources are necessary in order to prove the Bible correct, but they can be utilized as tools in helping us to understand a little better of what was going on in that culture at that time. Prophets were really no rarity in those days, whether pagan, false, or true. Other nations had prophets that would bring tidings from the gods, or a god, and the message was given to elicit a response from the people.

Guidelines for Interpretation

Guilt plays a major role, even today, and guilt was a tool used by prophets in order to bring about change. However, guilt in itself cannot be used just "because the prophets did it." No, strict means must be put on the biblical text, and rather than use a text as a club, the preacher ought to rightly divide it and follow the correct model of the prophet—not only the judging side of that model. In order to interpret these texts properly, careful study must be made.

1. Announcement of judgment came in a specific historical situation based on a specific word from God.
2. Announcement of judgment rested on firm historical evidence that God's people had developed a lifestyle that ignored God and broke that people's covenant commitments.
3. Announcement of judgment resulted in widely differing responses.
4. Announcement of judgment does not try to get something out of the people to benefit the preacher or congregation.
5. Announcement of judgment "in itself brings the hearers (or a third party) under judgment..."
6. Announcement of judgment does not entrap God.
7. Announcement of judgment is only a part of the prophetic message, and, indeed, the introductory part.

Conclusion

Jeremiah at times used an emotional draw in order to communicate God's message. These messages came with a clear intention in mind, and the manner in which they were delivered brought clarity, and emotional understandability.

1 P. 163

2 P. 164

Lament

Introduction

We sometimes think sorrow is sin. At times we associate sadness with a lack of joy, and the fruit of the spirit do not include lament. The Bible however, the Old Testament in particular, is riddled with laments, and the presupposed ideas we may have had about the term lament may not be as well-founded as we may have thought. Many Bible scholars have puzzled over texts of Scripture that do not seem to jive well with other texts, and specifically the laments have been a source of ulcers for a few who cannot grasp certain facts.

What Is a Lament?

Let us first view the Psalms. Grouped in the Psalms, as this author suggests, are three major categories: Psalms of orientation, disorientation, and reorientation. The titles are somewhat self-explanatory, but in relation to our subject, orientation is a direct praise of God, with no problems, basically. Disorientation is the major section that we are dealing with, in that something has come between a right relationship, and the poet is baring his heart. The last group is reorientation, and those are Psalms of restored fellowship where the prayers have been heard and answered, allowing for thanks from the author. Of these three groups are a few more groups relating to the laments within them: individual, communal, and royal laments. These are simply the ones from whom the lament is originating.

How the Psalmist Expresses Lament

A general read can tell you a lot about what genre the text is written in, but a deeper look at lament reveals a certain structure—though not rigid and unmovable.

1. Invocation. A plea to one who is far greater—the only one who can help in a situation that is out of any human's control. Addressed to God.

2. Plea to God for help. Usually in the imperative mood, as a sense of desperation.

3. Complaints. This is usually the motivating factor in the lament, and from this part of the text we learn about the heart of the individual.

4. Confession of sin or an assertion of innocence. The Bible speaks no lie, and if the author was repenting of a sin, he would bare his whole heart. If he were innocent, he here would express his innocence and plea for God to weigh the balance in their favor, as he promised in his covenant with His people. See, in their minds, again, the righteous were blessed, and the wicked were cursed. The only way for God to be vindicated in telling them that, to them, was for their enemies to suffer such a blow that they would be equal. On the flop side, for them to be suffering, to them it would seem that they were unrighteous, and almost a frustrated plea for God's righteousness to be revealed is the assertion of innocence.

5. *Curse of enemies.* Hard to understand at times, due to the harsh nature, but in reality, they expected God to work on their side and in their minds, the balance had to be equal between them as righteous children of God and the wicked generation.

6. *Confidence in God's response.*

7. *Hymn or blessing.* Often, the last two seem so abrupt because of the apparent change in disposition and thinking about the problem at hand. Almost always is there a turn from that which was the worst thing in the world at the time, to a realization of God, and a resulting abounding joy that brings forth praise.

To Whom the Psalmist Expresses Lament

Pretty much only three people "receive" a lament—it is directed toward an enemy, toward the lamenter, or toward God. The enemy is usually the one who is causing the distress that evokes the lament, and that is almost obvious. This enemy is not always named though; in fact, he is rarely ever named. The general nature of laments is such that can be applied to a wide variety of circumstances, and over periods of centuries. Second, the lamenter is seen, though not as often as the others, directing his lament toward himself. Whether through circumstances that were unfavorable, or sin, or a variety of other reasons, sometimes the author directs the lament at himself.

Last mentioned was the lament toward God. This is the most dangerous of the three, and yet sometimes this is the one we most can relate to. A wide variety of emotions are involved in all three, and a combination of two or all three can be seen in many different Psalms.

Where Laments Are Found

Lament in the Old Testament. Psalms is the most widely known and most abundant of the laments, but also the most often overlooked. The nature described above of the hymn or blessing at the end often lands the Psalm on a high note, rather than a melancholy sour note. This fact turns our attention to God, as it should, but also away from the lament aspect. Second, Lamentations is an obvious lament book, followed by Jeremiah. Many other books include portions of laments, all throughout the Old Testament, but the general view of each of these books would cause us to remember their lamentable nature.

Lament in the Near East. Outside the Bible, lament is seen in ancient literature dated at the same time as the major lament passages. This is no strange feat, in that God would have used language that the people could easily understand and relate with in familiarity, but that is not to say that the Bible in any way borrowed their literature for its own. Similarities have cause some scholars to believe that the biblical texts are somehow stolen, but in view of inspiration that cannot be the case.

Lament in the New Testament. Though there is not really a direct connection, links to the Old Testament can be found in the New Testament in the Gospels and the writings, i.e. Christ's lament over God's forsaking him.

How to Interpret Lament

1. Read the lament in its literary and historical context.
2. Apply the conventions of ancient Semitic poetry to lament.
3. Try to discover the reason for the lament.
4. Explore the theological teaching of the lament.
5. Reflect on the lament's appeal to our emotions and our will.

Conclusion

The author depicts Psalms 77 as a lament, bringing to light its high points in our outline above. It is a sad song, written in a time of personal or corporate trouble, and the negative emotions often triumph in the joy that the Father will come out on top in the end. The deep emotions turn to God—swapping lament for joy.

Praise

Introduction

"Praise the Lord!" we say, but do we really understand what lies behind all of that? I didn't. And I still feel as if I don't, but I know I understand it a little bit more now. This praise we speak about and read about in the Bible...how did it take place? Well, David in the Psalms would almost always either recognize God's attributes and extol Him for them or he would recognize God's marvelous dealings in his life. Psalms could be labeled, and they were for hundreds of years, in dozens of individual and separate topics and categories, but not until Hermann Gunkel came around in the early 1900's did anyone start to study the Psalms in relation to their function or form.

How the Psalmist Expresses Praise

Two ideas come to play in praise, one is reciting the attributes of God, and another is reciting the acts of God—a descriptive, and a declarative praise, respectively. Each brings the believer into closer fellowship with the Father, and he in turn blesses his people.

Praising God for who He is. (Descriptive Praise). Focusing on God, and proclaiming his wonderful nature is a great way to praise the Father. The word in the Hebrew from which we get the word hallelujah is used numerous times in the Old Testament in correlation to praise, and there are five subcategories of this praise.

1. *Hymns.* Known as the songs of Israel
2. *Enthronement psalms.* These are psalms which declare the heavenly nature and kingship of God and His rule.

3. *Songs of Zion, including pilgrim psalms.* These were probably sung on the way to Jerusalem on the journeys for the feasts.
4. *Royal psalms.* The acknowledging of the ultimate kingship of the Lord over the kings of the earth—written from the earthly king's perspective usually. These psalms were also messianic often, and consisted of an introduction, the main section, and the recapitulation—drawing everything to a closing praise. The call to praise, the cause for it, and the conclusions of it is seen in this little three-point deal.
5. Creation psalms.

Praising God for what He has done. (Declarative Praise). The answers to prayer and good tidings from the Lord deserve much thanks and praise, and the declaring of the facts as they are is a great means. These can be psalms of thanksgiving on an individual basis, or they can be a communal thanksgiving, but they too, like almost all praise, consist of the introduction, the main section, and the conclusion. The difficulty comes in trying to decide what type praise (or even what genre, for that matter) is being implemented.

Where Praise is Found in the Ancient Near East

Very common in the Eastern languages and writings were the praises to the false gods, but most praises were generally descriptive rather than declarative—in my opinion this is so because the prayers were probably rarely answered. Sample prayers of praise are given in the textbook, and ancient writings again do not have to be present in order for the Bible to be true—God's Word will stand.

How to Interpret Praise

1. Examine the parallelism that is typical of Hebrew poetry. There are many different types of parallelism, but they can be divided into three groups. Synonymous—that style in which one line complements the next; antithetical—when the two lines helpfully contrast one another; and synthetical—when one line builds upon, complement, or refine in some way the previous.

2. Allow for figurative language in the Hebrew poetry. Not seldom, word pictures are used to portray a vivid image in the mind, and often these words are not to be taken literally. To be likened to a tree, the sun, or a plant would not literally be complimentary, but in terms of strength and stamina they would be. Symbolism is present, but caution must be made so as not to take it too far.

3. Try to discover the historical occasion for the psalm being studied. Not always will you have the information, and not always will the psalm provide the necessary background—many are left vague on purpose—but for those you can understand, study it out.

4. Determine the type of psalm, whether it features descriptive praise or declarative praise and whether the praise is by an individual or the people as a whole.

5. Identify timeless spiritual principles that are valid and applicable to all people in the same or similar circumstances.

Conclusion

The author brought to light an interesting point in the life of Jonah, and related that the message that Jonah sent in the belly of the whale was not a lamenting passage at all, but rather a message of praise for the salvation of his body from the drowning in the sea. Without this praise the whole book would fall in two, and the lessons learned brought Jonah to a point of deeper worship of his Father. He brought to light all the major point discussed in the chapter, and concluded with a summary of what was said throughout. God gives us so much, and is so much, and our acknowledging of both those facts is what allows us to praise Him. He reminds us of all the warnings given in the chapter earlier, and closes with the fact that it is good to praise the Lord.

Selected Bibliography

1. Sandy, D. Brent; Giese, Ronald L. Jr.; *Cracking Old Testament Codes*; Broadman and Holman Publishers; Nashville, TN; 1995

Appendix 2

Sources

Sources For Ideas

The ideas for the structure, layout and format of this devotional book are derived from the following sources, although the exact structure is unique as what we are calling our BIBS model:

***My Biography of God*, by Sam Brock.** *My Biography of God* is a daily devotional set up in a one-week format. Each week the reader studies a certain passage every day and answers questions from the text that lead him to conclusions about God. The conclusions are written in various formats throughout the book, including attributes about God, names of God and more. *My Biography of God* is produced by *Iron Sharpeneth Iron*—the publication ministry of Ironwood Christian Camp.

***Living by the Book*, by Howard Hendricks.** *Living by the Book* is a book divided into clear sections emphasizing various Bible study techniques. The main idea borrowed from this book was that Bible study should be done in a sequence of observation, interpretation and application.

***How to Read the Bible for All Its Worth*, by Gordon Fee and Douglas Stewart.** *How to...* is an instructional book on interpreting various biblical genres.

***Biblical Preaching*, by Haddon Robinson.** *Biblical Preaching* is an instructional book on how to study the Bible in order to present a single concept (Big Idea) through preaching. Many examples in the BIBS explanations and appendices are taken from *Biblical Preaching*.

***Invitation to Biblical Preaching*, by Don Sunukjian.** *Invitation to Biblical Preaching* is an instructional book on how to study the Bible in order to present a single concept (Big Idea) through preaching. The main wording borrowed for the BIBS format are the questions: "What is God saying?" (Big Idea) and "What is God saying *to us*?" (application)

Disclaimer: The author does not necessarily endorse or agree with all doctrinal positions of each of these other authors. The aforementioned books are resources that contributed to forming the BIBS process.

Appendix 3

BIBS Devotional Book

A Snapshot

The BIBS Devotional book was developed by Calvary Baptist Church in 2012 as a way to provide Christians a daily Bible study program that allowed both deep and wide study of Scripture. The following pages include excerpts from the book and serve as a summary of the BIBS Devotional process.

B.I.B.S.
Big Idea Bible Study

These FOOLS
put my cape on
BACKWARDS!

THE BIBLE SPARES YOU
FROM THE MESSES
OF LIFE!

(Name)_____

The BIBS Devotional Book is a daily Bible reading and study plan. It is designed to guide the reader in both an in-depth study of a certain short passage every day, as well as weekly overview readings of the surrounding chapters to provide context.

Ryan Rench is the youth pastor at **Calvary Baptist Church** in Temecula, CA, Pastor W. M. Rench. He has been on staff since May, 2010, and was trained at Heartland Baptist Bible College in Oklahoma City, OK (BA, MM). He also interned under Pastor Wayne Hardy of Bible Baptist Church in Stillwater, OK.

Note from the author: "There are two main reasons I do not often use or recommend most devotional books or most things written for teens. First, they cater to this false idea that teens are somehow less intelligent and need things 'dumbed down' for them to get it. Wrong! Those in their teen years are highly motivated to excel at whatever they're challenged to do. BIBS simply challenges them to know their Bibles if they're up to it.

"Second, most devotionals have the reader read very little of the Bible and think very little for himself. Then, if there is a biblical text to read--and sometimes it is only one verse(!)--the devotional tells the reader what to think about that text. God's Word IS saying something in every text, but discovering it for myself and applying it to myself is much more lasting. Following the BIBS format offers both the depths of Scripture AND the flow of thought of the context of Scripture. It is a guide to help you hear from God and a tool to help you understand and apply His desires for your life."

B.I.B.S. Created in 2012. All quotations use the King James Bible.

The Bible is all that will matter...

Before getting into the BIBS book you have to first know that the Bible is the only thing that will matter to you in 246 years (random...). Or 1,000 years. It's the only thing that will protect you from the nasty messes in life. Seems crazy NOT to read it!

Personal discipline

Are you willing to develop the discipline of Bible study without someone forcing this on you? If so, this Bible study will be the best thing you do over the next few weeks. If not, this whole Bible study will be unneeded.

You'll commit to band, martial arts, sports practice or even school... but will you commit to stretch yourself spiritually? This Bible study will outlast ALL those other things in your life, so really take it seriously. At LEAST commit to <u>four full weeks</u>. That's only two cycles through the format we're using, and it could take as little as 15 minutes per day.

Commit now?

Maybe you will commit to the full devotional. Maybe you just want to commit to the first section. Will you commit right now?

3 STEPS

TO VIEW EVERY TEXT

Taken from Howard Hendricks' *Living By the Book*, each Bible text needs to be viewed three ways: OBSERVATION, INTERPRETATION, and APPLICATION. Bookmark or dog-ear these pages to refer back to them for the first few weeks. They'll help you when you're stuck for what to look for in your study.

OBSERVATION
THE BIRDS-EYE VIEW

INTERPRETATION
WHAT IS GOD SAYING?

APPLICATION
WHAT IS GOD SAYING TO ME?

# OBSERVATION

The birds-eye view

The first view, OBSERVATION, is the broad overview of what's going on in the text. It's as if you're flying way up in the sky and surveying the whole land (although I doubt this fat little bird can fly!). Ask broad questions:

- Why was the book written in the first place?
- What happened in this story before this text?
- To whom is it written?
- What's the problem with mankind that God is trying to fix with this text? (It HAS to address some need... what is it?)
- What *type* of writing is it?
  - Narrative – A broad, often long story with a lesson or moral.
  - Law – God's commandments for His people Israel.
  - Prophets – Warnings from God to His people Israel.
  - Psalms – Songs and prayers to or about God.
  - Wisdom – Proverbs and poetry.
  - Gospels – The story of Christ from different perspectives.
  - Acts – A history of the church in transition.
  - Parable – A story with a single point.
  - Epistle – A letter to a church or individual.
  - Prophecy – Foretelling of judgments and hope.
  - For more information on genres, see **Appendix 2.**

Interpretation

What is God saying?

The second view, INTERPRETATION, answers the basic question, "What is God saying?" If God said things that meant something to them (the original readers), what was He saying? In the Bible characters' terms, what was God fixing or teaching or encouraging or commanding *them* to do? If we know what God *said*, we can know what God is *saying*. You've already got a good start through OBSERVATION, but now let's go deeper by learning INTERPRETATION.

Read

Your best tool will be reading. Read through the text (the small "chunk" of Scripture) and try to get a broad idea of what it's saying.

Reread

Now, go back and read those few verses again. Think harder this time. Try to get an overall idea of what's going on.

Tools of the trade

Some good tools for observation and interpretation are a simple Bible reference tool for your computer, a Bible dictionary and/or a study Bible. Free Bible software can be downloaded at www.e-sword.net. Or, several online sources such as classic.net.bible.org will have Strongs reference numbers under the King James tab. Good dictionaries such as Webster's 1828 can be downloaded

Flag Words

You'll come across words you don't understand, key words or repeating words through your reading. Either mark them and come back, or get your tools out and look them up as you go. The King James is not difficult to understand... you just need a couple tools to help along the way.

"WHAT AM I TALKING ABOUT?"

You're trying to answer the question, "What am I talking about?" What's this text about overall? Don't get lost in all the little details... think BIG idea.

If the BIG IDEA is like a tree, then lets just start with the main part--the trunk. This is the trunk. "What am I talking about?" Start broadly:

Word

You've read and reread. You've looked up confusing words and noticed repeating words. Now **what one word comes to mind as an overall thought** for this text? (Please see Appendix 3 for examples.)

Phrase

Now, suppose that one word is *Praise*. **Narrow that down** a little. Is this text saying everything about praise? No. Whose praise? Who is praising? What about praise? What kind? There

for free through E-Sword. Further, a good study Bible will give you an overview of the book before you begin reading; and it will give you helpful insights such as cross references, maps and further explanations as you are reading through a text.

Warning: use man's wisdom sparingly! Your goal is to hear from God directly, so don't rely on these Bible study tools as a crutch to "get the right answer." You're not after the "right answer." You are after hearing from God, so spend most of your time in His Word!

are a lot of directions this could go!

Suppose (as you see from our example in Appendix 3) our phrase then becomes *Praise of God*. That narrows it down, but it's still not enough. We all know a lot about praising God. What about it?! Go further...

Sentence

Now, **expand that phrase into a sentence.** What about praising God? Who should? Don't come up with the sentence on your own. Base it on the text.

If you could boil this text down into a sentence, *what is this text talking about?*

Suppose, again from our example, that the sentence is "We should praise the Lord." That's a full sentence -- a complete thought. It is definite. It is concise. It is a rock.

ROCKS
It is easier to catch a rock than a handful of sand. The Bible is not full of a bunch of unrelated thoughts (sand). It is full of ideas... rocks!

Summary

In summary, the way to answer the question "What am I talking about?" is to follow this progression:

- Read
- Reread
- Flag Words
- Boil Down to a Word
- Expand to a Phrase
- Summarize in a Sentence

"WHAT AM I SAYING ABOUT WHAT I'M TALKING ABOUT?"

If the BIG IDEA is a tree and we've already found the trunk, lets fill in all the branches -- all the little details that describe or enhance the trunk. These "branches" are all the details that say stuff about what we're talking about.

Question word

If you could turn your sentence into a question, what **question word** would you use? Is this a **who, what, where, when, why** or **how** text?

Question

OK, once you've found your word, **turn your sentence into a question.** For our running example, our sentence was:

"We should praise the Lord."

If our question word is *why*, then our question now is:

"**Why** should we praise the Lord?"

Answer(s)

Once you have the basic question, simply **answer it from the text.** These answers will fill out your tree with all the leaves and branches.

Why should we praise the Lord? Well, there are two answers, or two branches:

- Because his merciful kindness is great toward us.
- Because the truth of the Lord endureth forever.

Application

What is God saying *to me*?

There's only one *interpretation* to each passage--there's only one right answer to what God *said*. BUT... when it comes to APPLICATION (what God is *saying* to me) there are tons of ways this could go!

Overall, what did you learn?

God speaks in SO many different ways through His Word, and maybe He spoke to you from one little phrase, the whole "Big Idea," or even just in one word you studied. God is always speaking through His Word, so how did He speak to you through this text? How does it apply to you? What did you learn from it? How has it helped? How has it encouraged you? What did it challenge you to do?

Application days

Here's where we get to the hard part. It's easy to learn stuff about God. It's easy to know you're supposed to watch your mouth, guard your mind, be in church, give the gospel, care for others, obey your parents...

Those Bible truths are easy to know, but HARD to live. Every "Application Day" will need to be a serious time between you and God. First, pray and ask Him to reveal hidden sin. Next, ask Him to help you overcome it. Finally, ask Him if there's even anything small in your life that could be changed. He will reveal "big" and "small" sins in your life, and it is your job to change them through His power.

"Application Days" come around a couple times per week in the BIBS format. While you will be learning and growing **every day**, the "Application Day" should especially be a clear-minded, open-hearted soul searching time before God.

Self deception

But be ye doers of the word and not hearers only, **deceiving your own selves.** *James 1:22*

According to James 1:22, the more you hear the Word and don't do anything about it, the more self-deceived you become. That's scary... you don't even know *right now* if you're deceived (otherwise you wouldn't be deceived!).

DO something!

Determine to not ONLY know stuff about the Bible but to actually do stuff with your knowledge. If the "Big Idea" you find is something like, "Paul's desire to see the Thessalonians walk worthy drove him to self sacrifice," you can respond a couple different ways:

> *"That's nice. Paul sacrificed for others. What a swell guy. Time for me to go to school!"*

Or...

> *"Wow. Paul was so passionate about helping others, he sacrificed a lot. How have I* **sacrificed** *lately? I really haven't. Maybe I should.*
>
> *"What can I sacrifice?! I'm only a teen! What do I have to give in self-sacrifice?*
>
> *"Well, I guess I DO have a little* **money.** *It's not much, but I know I need to sacrifice something, so I'm going to start giving to missions every week by faith.*
>
> *"I don't have much, but I DO have some spare* **time.** *I waste a lot on video games. I doubt Paul did that. I need to spend my time better. I'm going to limit my video games to 1 hour and spend the rest of the time on my devotions (or exercise, or writing notes, or...)*
>
> *"I don't have much experience, but I CAN* **work.** *I want to donate my youth and my energy to help out wherever I can. Not for payment but to simply serve. I'll call the church today to see where I can work."*

Make a plan

Once you've decided to do something, write out your plan. **Be specific.**

So that I am not deceived, I plan to:

> *"Sacrifice by committing to $2/week.*
>
> *"Time my video games and stop at one hour total. I'll spend the spare time doing my chores, reading _____, writing encouraging notes to _____, and exercising for ____ minutes per day.*
>
> *"I'm going to call my youth pastor and set up a time to do yard work around the church. I'll also ask him this week at church if there's anything I can do throughout the week."*

Specifically, what is one thing you can do this week that will be acting on what you've learned from God's Word?

Conclude in prayer

God's been speaking and you've been responding by promising to act on His Word. Now conclude in prayer and ask God's help and strength as you do what you committed to do. (Dan. 1:8)

Notes:

DAILY CHECKLIST

The following list is the basic idea for how each day will look. Certain days will have lined sections to write on, and other days will be very simple and short. Cycle 2 Week 2 will only have one Application Day and no Observation Day and certain other weeks may vary. Each step is explained further each day.

 THURSDAY Reading Day (Observation)
1. Pray
2. Study Bible – read intro paragraph
3. Read whole book (or large portion)
4. Note text 1 & 2

 FRIDAY Rereading Day
1. Read 2 chapters
2. Reread text 1
3. One word
4. Phrase

 SATURDAY Thinking Day (Interpretation)
1. Read 2 chapters
2. Reread text 1
3. Review yesterday's phrase
4. Expand to a sentence (tree trunk)
5. Turn it into a question (what question word?)
6. Answer the question (branches)

 SUNDAY Application Day (Application)
1. Read full chapter
2. Combine "Trunk" and "Branches"
3. What is God saying? (BIG IDEA - full tree)
4. What is God saying TO ME? Application.
5. Write plan

🔍 MONDAY Rereading Day

1. Read 2 chapters
2. Reread text 2
3. One word
4. Phrase

TUESDAY Thinking Day (Interpretation)

1. Read 2 chapters
2. Reread text 2
3. Review yesterday's phrase
4. Expand to a sentence (tree trunk)
5. Turn it into a question (what question word?)
6. Answer the question (branches)

👤 WEDNESDAY Application Day (Application)

1. Read full chapter
2. Combine "Trunk" and "Branches"
3. What is God saying? (BIG IDEA - full tree)
4. What is God saying TO ME? Application.
5. Write plan
6. Discuss texts 1 & 2 in church

Ready to get going? *God, please help us as we learn your will through your Word.*

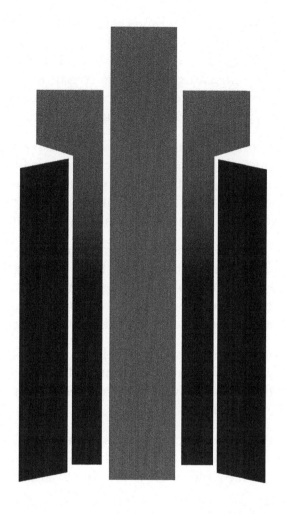

CALVARY BAPTIST PUBLICATIONS

TEMECULA, CA | CALVARYBAPTIST.PUB

EVERY NOW AND THEN, Dad and I get a little burst of inspiration to write. We jot a few notes down, work up an outline, and then hammer out a rough--I mean *rough*--draft. The secretaries and other proofers in our church make the rough draft sound nice, and then we print them up for our church people as a pamphlet, a brochure, a minibook, a booklet, or a fully formatted book.

All our writing projects started as a way to help our church in some way. Ministering on a weekly schedule produces loads of content on tons of different topics, and we have worked to capture some of that content into formats that can last longer than the one sermon, seminar or conference that they originated from.

Maybe you or the people in your home church have faced some of the same issues that we have faced here. We all ask the same questions and seek The Book for the right answers. Maybe one of the resources that we have put together can help you answer some of your questions or tackle some of the issues you might be facing.

We do not write because we want to sell a ton of books. We write because we want to formulate certain philosophies, doctrines, reasons, and thoughts into words so that people can understand them and take them home.

If these can be a help to you, please **let us know** and we would be glad to give you one **free**. If you would like to order any of these in **bulk (five or more)**, please email me directly at **RyanRench@ gmail.com**.

I would love it if any of these books helped you in *any* way. Seriously!

Living to serve,

Ryan Rench

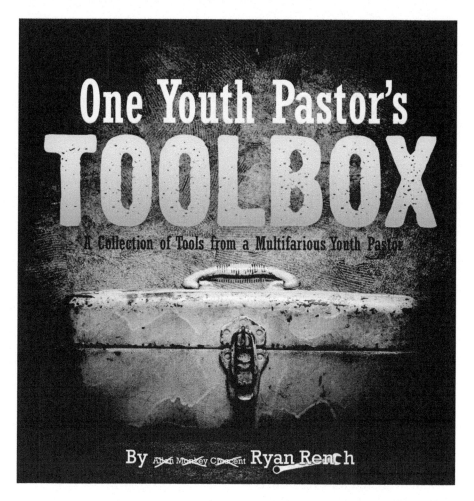

One Youth Pastor's
TOOLBOX

A Collection of Tools from a Multifarious Youth Pastor

By ~~Aaron Monkey Crescent~~ Ryan Rench

A good toolbox is full of a man's favorite tools.... even if he doesn't use them all the time. They need to be in there.

As a youth pastor, I feel the same way about my ministry tools. I have a few goodies that stay close by me, and others that I know are perfect for certain situations.

I've tested them out. I've tried them. They've worked for me. Some more than others, but ALL have helped in some way.

After testing them on my teens for 6 years and sharing the results at an annual youth leaders retreat, I decided to compile the ideas here. Steal what you like. Adapt what you want. File the rest for later. Enjoy!

183 pages. Available on Amazon.com. $11.99

BIBS

BIG IDEA BIBLE STUDY

The pastor says, "You need to be in God's Word," but your eyes glaze over every time you open a book—any book—and you do not understand the Bible.

"Yeah right," you think. "It doesn't make sense to me."

It does not have to be that way. You can read the Bible AND understand what it says.

It takes a format that works for you.

That is what this book is all about. BIBS (Big Idea Bible Study) is a format designed for every Christian. It is a Bible study method that takes you into the depths of Scripture but also keeps sight of the bigger picture.

BIBS is a simple step-by-step course to help you discover what God is saying in His Word. You will learn to observe, interpret and apply Scriptural truth, taking the "old, dry, boring" book and discovering the life it promises for your soul.

226 pages. *Available on Amazon.com.* **$13.99**

HOW TO **READ** AND **UNDERSTAND** YOUR BIBLE
USING OBSERVATION, INTERPRETATION & APPLICATION

BIBS
BIG IDEA BIBLE STUDY

RYAN RENCH
FOREWORD BY: SAM DAVISON

BIBS Daily Devotional

The *BIBS Daily Devotional* is a daily Bible reading and study plan. It is designed to guide the reader in both an in-depth study of a certain short passage every day, as well as weekly overview readings of the surrounding chapters to provide context.

Note from the author: "There are two main reasons I do not often use or recommend most devotional books or most things written for teens. First, they cater to this false idea that teens are somehow less intelligent and need things 'dumbed down' for them to get it. Wrong! Those in their teen years are highly motivated to excel at whatever they are challenged to do. BIBS simply challenges them to know their Bibles if they are up to it.

"Second, most devotionals have the reader read very little of the Bible and think very little for himself. Then, if there is a biblical text to read--and sometimes it is only one verse(!)--the devotional tells the reader what to think about that text. God's Word IS saying something in every text, but discovering it for myself and applying it to myself produces more lasting results. Following the BIBS format offers both the depths of Scripture AND the flow of thought of the context of Scripture. It is a guide to help you hear from God and a tool to help you understand and apply His desires for your life."

INTERNING WELL
A collection of articles to help church interns

INTERNS ARE MORE THAN GOPHERS ("go for" this and "go for" that). At least, they should be. An intern should learn as much as possible through the experience of ministering to others—church staff and church members.

This book was birthed from our daily intern staff meetings. I was never a summer intern, but I was a staff intern for two years under Pastor Wayne Hardy (Bible Baptist Church, Stillwater, OK). I try to cram my two years into the 12 weeks with our interns. Poor guys. After each activity or event, we discuss the details and provide training. Sometimes the training is instruction, correction or rebuke. Sometimes it is embarrassing. Sometimes it is awkward. All of it, though, is intended to edify—to strengthen and build up—the intern. It is intended to create a ministry-minded, servant-hearted future church staff member.

As an intern, learn as much as you can. Do all you can to be a blessing and help to others. Serve. Lead. Grow. Change. INTERN WELL. *190 pages. Available on Amazon.com $12.99*

A CASE FOR BIBLE COLLEGE
Why Our Church Encourages Our Graduates To Attend For At Least One Year

I have talked to people who think Bible College is a waste of time. If that is you, please read this book; especially PART ONE.

I have also talked with prospective students who have NO idea what to expect when they get there. If you plan to attend Bible College, please read this book; especially PART TWO.

PART ONE builds a case for why many churches encourage high school graduates to attend at least one year of Bible College. It details benefits, considers objections and discusses biblical principles on choosing a Bible college.

PART TWO will prepare you—the prospective student—for the distinct new culture of Bible College. It will help you anticipate the spiritual, academic and social changes that will take place in your first year.

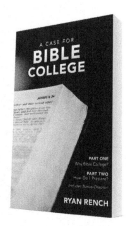

The BONUS CHAPTER at the end is written specifically to those students who have chosen to attend Heartland Baptist Bible College in Oklahoma City. This chapter provides a quick look at a few Heartland-specific topics that may not apply to other Bible colleges.

188 pages. Available on Amazon.com $12.99

A CASE FOR BEING
TIMELESS

DO YOU WANT TO BE A LAB RAT?

I don't. Who would?

But that is exactly what the youth of today are: lab rats. Modern church leaders use the youth--not the elderly--as their lab rats. New church fads are tested on those who have not lived very long.

New is not always bad... but it is always new. It is never time-tested. It is never "tried and true."

We never know if "new" will work, because it does not have a history.

Before trusting the new fads that sweep through modern churches, I want to anchor my beliefs to something TIMELESS. I want to know that that the path I am on has proved to be right. I don't want to be a lab rat. Do your tests on someone else.

I choose to be TIMELESS.

150 pages. Available on Amazon.com $9.99

NO TIME TO READ?
LISTEN INSTEAD
audiobooks available from Audible.com

You might think, "I don't have time to read." Do you **jog**, have a long **commute**, or do **housecleaning** or **yardwork**?

If so, listen to audiobooks! Many of Calvary Baptist Church's resources are available in **audiobook** format, professionally narrated and produced through Audible.com, an Amazon company.

Scan for titles on Audible.com

Print and ebooks on Amazon.com

MINIBOOKS
"A CASE FOR" SERIES

A CASE FOR... is a growing series of minibooks designed to help the reader find **biblical and practical reasons** for various doctrines and practices he might find in the church he attends. None of the minibooks are meant to be exhaustive resources on any of the topics. Rather, each minibook serves as a collection of **logical and reasonable arguments** in favor of each biblical topic. They are written in **easy-to-read language** and are short enough to complete in one sitting.

Visit **www.cbctemecula.org** for more information or to order bulk quantities. The A CASE FOR... series includes several minibooks:

A CASE FOR DATING GOD'S WAY

Hoping to save teens a lot of future heartache, this minibook was written to help navigate some of life's questions on biblical dating. Should I date? How do I start? Read the book to find out!

e-book

audiobook

A CASE FOR SUNDAY EVENING CHURCH

"Weeell... attendance is down so we'll just cancel our Sunday night services." Should you? This minibook gives a few solid reasons why our church still believes in the Sunday evening service.

e-book

audiobook

A Case For Reverence

Most church services today are very casual, laid back and relaxed. This minibook builds a strong case for conducting church services in more of a reverent, respectful attitude.

e-book

audiobook

A Case For Saturday Soul-Winning

Every Saturday our church goes into the community to spread the gospel through our door-to-door soul-winning program. While our main focus is on obeying the Great Commission, several other factors are at play each week, as well. Read our minibook for good reasons to have an outreach program.

Printed version only available at Calvary Baptist Church. Call to order.

A Case For Why We Have "Church"

"Where did this whole 'church' thing come from, anyway? What about para-church organizations? Aren't all churches the same?" Read this minibook to find out.

print edition

all printed

BOOKLETS

BY PASTOR W. M. RENCH

Islam. Around the time that Muslims were seeking to build a mosque near Ground Zero, ground-breaking ceremonies were beginning on the 5-acre plot of land next door to our church for another Mosque. Pastor Rench was on CNN discussing the effects of Islam on America, and wrote this followup booklet to highlight some of Islam's teachings from their Quran.

Enduring Sound Doctrine. At times, error creeps into churches through outside influences. A pastor that cares for his sheep will warn against false doctrine, encouraging the flock to "endure sound doctrine," as Paul taught. This booklet details some of the errors of home churches, the Pearl family, and others who lift certain teachings above the importance of the church.

Skip the Sermon, Worship at Home? In our area of Southern California, and with the prevalence on online and other media options for church, some Christians are convinced that home worship is the same as church worship. This booklet gives several warnings against home church gatherings that are replacing the assemblies of people in true churches.

Classic Christianity. Pastor Rench received an advertisement in the mail promoting another rock concert. He remembered his past with rock music with shame. To his surprise, the advertisement was for a church, although the appearance was worldly. This booklet contrasts classic, timeless Christianity against the modern, changing fads of today's contemporary Christianity.

Is Sunday School Biblical? A hot topic among home-church advocates these days is, "Is Sunday School biblical?" The question is sincere. While Sunday School is certainly not *anti*-biblical (there's no clear teaching *against* it directly), to say that it is *un*-biblical (in that it's not even mentioned) is also incorrect. This booklet shows the biblical precedent of Sunday School.

Calvary Chapel: What's the Difference? Our church is often mistaken with a church called Calvary Chapel, a non-denominational church with several locations and schools across Southern California. Because of the confusion between our church and theirs, Pastor Rench clarifies the differences in Bible doctrines and practices.

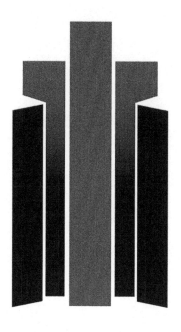

CALVARY
BAPTIST
PUBLICATIONS

TEMECULA, CA | CALVARYBAPTIST.PUB

31087 Nicolas Rd.
Temecula, CA 92591
(951) 676-8700

Made in the USA
Monee, IL
10 September 2020